A Life of Faith

21 Days to Overcoming Fear and Doubt

Shelley Hitz

A Life of Faith: 21 Days to Overcoming Fear and Doubt

© 2014 Body and Soul Publishing

ISBN-13: 978-0615989693
ISBN-10: 0615989691

Published by Body and Soul Publishing
Printed in the United States of America

Join our Facebook group and learn more information at:
www.facebook.com/groups/21daysoffaith

Table of Contents

Introduction

Faith. What is the first thing that comes to your mind when you think of the word faith? I often think of faith as stepping out into the unknown, the evidence of things not seen, and ultimately giving up my control.

One example of faith is jumping off a high dive. My husband, CJ, tells a story of his first experience with the high dive when he was only eight or nine years old. In that phase of his life he loved going to the public swimming pool in his small town in the summer with his friends. As is common with most public pools, his pool had both a low dive and a high dive. One day, giving in to peer pressure, he decided to jump off of the high dive for the first time. Even today, he admits that he has a healthy fear of heights. However, on that particular summer day, his fear of heights got the best of him. As he climbed the ladder of the notorious high dive and saw how far he had to jump, fear took over. He stood on the high dive and contemplated whether or not he wanted to take the risk and jump. Ultimately, taking that step of faith would mean giving up his control and overcoming his fear. However, even with all his friends watching, he chickened out and slowly climbed back down the ladder of the high dive to the jeering of his friends.

Haven't we all experienced something like this in our lives as well? A moment where we have to decide if we are willing to step out in faith.

1

The good news about this story is that it does not end there. Later that day, CJ mustered up the courage to try the high dive once again. And this time, despite his fear, he jumped. And you know what happened? He loved it! Not only did he land safely in the water without injury, he also experienced the thrill of his lifetime. He then proceeded to jump off the high dive repeatedly for the rest of the day. In fact, he says eventually he became so daring that he would do all kinds of tricks off the high dive, including a one and a half twist dive.

What a great illustration of faith! Jumping off a high dive is simply one picture of stepping out in faith and the joy that comes as a result.

21 Days of Faith Challenge...

This year, I want to live a life of faith. I want my faith to be more than simply saying "I believe in God." I want it to be real...a genuine faith that overflows from a heart that is fully trusting in God in every area of my life.

Do You Have Faith?

To be honest, my knee-jerk reaction to this question would be a confident, "Yes!" Why? Well, I have been a Christian for over 20 years. And as a Christian, faith is the foundation of everything I believe.

I grew up as a "PK" (Pastor's Kid) and first surrendered my life to Christ at seven years old. However, I drifted during high school during a rebellious season in my life. I partied, drank to get drunk, and started down a path of destruction. Alcoholism runs on both sides of my family. And so I firmly believe that if God had not intervened, I could have also ended up on that same path. However, through circumstances that I see now as God's intervention in my life, we moved during the middle of my junior year in high school. For the first time, I met other teens that were truly living for Christ in my new school in Findlay Ohio. And their faith in God was not something they were doing for their parents or to look good. It was real. God used these new Christian friends and an organization called Youth for Christ (YFC) to impact my life for eternity. At a YFC event near the end of my junior year in 1992, I decided to live my life for Christ. I cannot explain the change in my life any other way except that God intervened. I was rescued. In fact, as I recall these events, I have tears of gratitude in my eyes for God's mercy on my life. I firmly believe my life would have turned out so much differently had we not moved during my junior year. What I thought would ruin my life, actually saved it.

And so, I have been on this journey of faith in God for over 20 years. Of course I believe in God and have faith. Right?

However, I have to admit that I have struggled with faith lately.

My Struggles with Doubt and Worry

I cannot pinpoint when it happened. But, gradually over the last 18 months, my thoughts began to change from faith in God to doubt. As circumstances in my life turned out much differently than I thought, I became disillusioned and started to wonder if God really had my best interests in mind.

Instead of trusting God with the circumstances of my life, I tried to take things into my own hands. As you can imagine, this led to worry. Worry, worry, and more worry. And as a result, I spent more time doubting God and worrying than I did in believing God and trusting Him with my life.

Ouch.

And with the worry and doubt, came a darkness over my life. Over the last year, I have felt depressed more often than I want to admit. And each time it would come, it felt like I would sink deeper into it.

This is when God led me to do the "*21 Days of Gratitude Challenge*." And it helped. But, I still felt the darkness settle over me. As I prayed, I realized that it was time to take the next step. It was time for a new challenge. It was time for me to allow God to replace the worry and doubt with trust and faith.

A Year of Faith

And so I sense that this year is to be a year of faith. As I start this *21 Days of Faith Challenge*, I know that I need God to empower me to change. I have formed bad habits of worry that I know I cannot change on my own. It will take an empowerment of the Holy Spirit and yet I am willing and ready to cooperate with Him. I am tired of worrying. I am tired of riding a rollercoaster of emotions that jerks me up and down, up and down. I am ready for this next step of faith.

Will You Join Me?

What about you? Will you consider joining me in these *21 Days of Faith*? Are you ready to surrender your worries and doubts to God? I have to warn you that this journey will not be easy. But, it will be worth it.

God often speaks to me in illustrations. The picture I see of myself right now is similar to someone who has gotten out of shape physically and is now 40 pounds overweight. After forming bad habits of not exercising and eating junk food, you have to reach a breaking point and be ready to change.

Exercising and eating right will not be easy, but it will be worth it.

And in a similar way, I have allowed myself to get out of shape spiritually. I have gained 40 pounds of worry and doubt and have formed bad habits. I am now at a breaking point and am ready to change. Trusting God and believing Him will not be easy, but it will be worth it.

Prayer Changes Things

Prayer changes things. It changes me. When I pray consistently to God something changes within me. However, sometimes it is easy to get caught up in the busyness of life and not take the time to pray.

We do not have to pray in a certain way for God to hear us. We can simply lift up the prayer of our hearts to Him as if we are talking with a friend. However, in this book, I have used examples of faith found in scripture and reworded them into prayers. Combining prayer with God's Word is powerful. I have experienced this in my own life and now want to share it with you.

They say it takes 21 days to form a new habit. And so I have shared 21 prayers of faith with you to help you form a habit of prayer in your life. I pray that these prayers help you to overcome fear and doubt by applying the power of prayer and God's Word to your life. I also pray that when you finish this book, your prayers will continue on your own. I encourage you to dig into God's Word and come up with your own prayers. If you are struggling in a certain area, I recommend using a concordance or an online tool like BibleGateway.com or BlueLetterBible.org to find scriptures on that topic and then reword them into prayers from your own heart.

In this book you will also read 21 different stories of faith from various authors. Sometimes the stories may focus on coming to faith in Christ for the first time. Other stories share lessons learned about faith during a difficult time.

Ultimately, we hope and pray that God uses these stories to inspire and encourage you in your own walk of faith. That by reading this book, your eyes will be fixed on Jesus, the author and perfecter of your faith, (Hebrews 12:2) allowing Him to strengthen your faith. Because *"without faith it is impossible to please Him, for he who comes to God must believe that He is, and that He is a rewarder of those who diligently seek Him."* ~Hebrews 11:6 (NKJV)

Ready to get started? Let's start with a prayer...

Lord, today I want to thank You for your grace and forgiveness. I confess that I struggle with worry and doubt. Please forgive me for not believing and trusting You. I am ready to change. Empower me with Your Holy Spirit to renew my mind with Your truth and change my thoughts from worry and doubt to thoughts of faith and trust. I thank You for Your unconditional love. Even though I have strayed from the path You have for me, You love me and accept me. Jesus, walk with me as I take this 21 days of faith challenge. I pray that I will not be the same person when it is over but instead a person living a life of faith.

Lord I thank You for each person who reads this book and lifts up these prayers to You. I pray that You would do a mighty work in their hearts as they spend these next 21 days in prayer with You. Change them from the inside out through Your Word and prayer. Give them a hunger and thirst for You that will continue past the last page of this book. We love You and thank You for this opportunity to come to You with our prayers of faith. Amen.

"Pray without ceasing."

~ I Thessalonians 5:17

"Ask, and it will be given to you; seek, and you will find; knock, and it will be opened to you."

~ Matthew 7:7

"Be anxious for nothing, but in everything by prayer and supplication, with thanksgiving, let Your requests be made known to God; and the peace of God, which surpasses all understanding, will guard Your hearts and minds through Christ Jesus."

~ Philippians 4:6-7

Day #1

Today is the first day of the faith challenge. Honestly, I feel like I am standing on the edge of a diving board getting ready to jump off. I am both excited and nervous as I commit to taking this challenge. However, one of the first questions we need to ask ourselves is simply, *"What is faith?"*

Personally, when I think of the word faith, many definitions come to mind. Here are just a few:

- A belief in God
- Stepping out into the unknown
- My thoughts and beliefs
- And so on

I think it would be interesting to ask 100 people this same question, *"What is faith?"* I am pretty sure there would be MANY different answers depending on each person's background, experiences, and Biblical knowledge. So as we get started, let's look at what the Bible says about faith. To do so, we will look at a well-known scripture from Hebrews 11:1.

"Now faith is the substance of things hoped for, the evidence of things not seen." (NKJV)

From this verse, we see that faith is defined in two ways:

#1: The substance of things hoped for and
#2: The evidence of things not seen

I also like the way the Amplified version says it.

"Now faith is the assurance (the confirmation, the title deed) of the things [we] hope for, being the proof of things [we] do not see and the conviction of their reality [faith perceiving as real fact what is not revealed to the senses]."

~ Hebrews 11:1 (AMP)

Did you catch that? If not, I encourage you to read it again. It says faith is the confirmation or the title deed of the things we hope for.

I am a visual person that learns best through illustrations and so I like how the Amplifed version says that faith is the title deed. Dictionary.com defines title deed as a "deed or document constituting evidence of ownership." Therefore, our faith is like a document that gives evidence of ownership of the things we hope for and those things we do not see. Let's take the illustration a bit further. Faith is like purchasing a home that I have never seen. Even though I have never seen the property or the house, the title deed proves that I am the owner and I can rest confidently in that knowledge.

Martin Luther King Jr. says it this way, *"Faith is taking the first step even when you can't see the whole staircase."*

Are you ready to live life this way? Trusting God even when you can't see how it will all work out. If so, you will truly be living out a life of faith.

The Faith Challenge:

> ➤ Write out Hebrews 11:1 and post it somewhere that you will see it every day throughout this challenge. Read it out loud and meditate on it.

> I encourage you to start a journal that you can write in each day. In your journal, write out what faith means to you. Compare it to the definition we studied in Hebrews 11:1. Are they similar, different? Ask God to reveal to you His definition of faith through His Word.

> For encouragement and accountability in your journey of faith, join our private Facebook group here: www.facebook.com/groups/21daysoffaith

Prayer of Faith:
Noah

Lord, I need You today. There are things in my life that just don't make sense. Help me to trust You even when I don't understand all the details or see how everything will turn out.

This reminds me of Noah and how You asked him to build an ark. You asked him to do something that did not make sense. His friends must have thought he was crazy for building a giant boat when it never rained. And yet he had faith in what You asked him to do and trusted You. He walked faithfully with You and this resulted in his family being saved.

Empower me to trust You in a deeper way today, Lord. Help me to walk faithfully with you and obey You even when it doesn't make sense. Thank You for drawing me closer to You today. I love you. In Jesus' name I pray, Amen.

"Noah was a righteous man, blameless among the people of his time, and he walked faithfully with God."
~ Genesis 6:9 (NIV)

"By faith Noah, being divinely warned of things not yet seen, moved with godly fear, prepared an ark for the saving of his household, by which he condemned the world and became heir of the righteousness which is according to faith."
~ Hebrews 11:7 (NKJV)

Also read: Genesis 6:9-22, 7:1-24

Story of Faith: An Unexpected Gift
CJ Hitz

"And God will generously provide all you need. Then you will always have everything you need and plenty left over to share with others."
~ 2 Corinthians 9:8 (NLT)

Upon getting married in August of 1998, my wife Shelley and I were staring at a total of $58,000 in school loans between both of us. Fortunately, Shelley had secured a position as a Physical Therapist which would ease our financial burden while I finished my student teaching.

My teaching certification would be Secondary Ed. Social Studies which would allow me to teach History, Geography, Sociology, Psychology and Government. These are subjects I enjoyed growing up and I knew I could also enjoy teaching them to middle and high schoolers. But over the next few months, I began noticing a change in my desires. My zeal for planning and preparing 7th grade History lessons was slowly diminishing while my heart's passion was to study the Bible.

I found myself looking forward to finishing a History lesson so I could get back to devouring God's Word. My supervising teacher noticed this and sat me down to have a talk. I admitted

11

to him that I hadn't devoted my best energy in preparing those lessons but I wasn't sure how I should handle this inner struggle. We both agreed that regardless of which direction I would go, I needed to stay focused and finish strong in my student teaching. Looking back, I'm thankful for the patience this outstanding teacher showed me.

After completing my teaching degree in November, I began doing some substitute teaching to bring in some extra income while seeking the Lord's direction for my life. As I was driving through town one day, I noticed a building with a sign that read, "Youth For Christ." I had first heard about this parachurch organization while taking a youth ministry class while at Anderson University. Still, I wasn't really familiar with what it was they did. After some deliberation, I decided to stop in and find out. "Certainly can't hurt," I thought to myself.

Paul, the Executive Director, greeted me at the door with enthusiasm. He invited me into his office where he proceeded to answer any questions I had while also introducing me to some of the staff. Their main mission and goal was to help lead students into a life-changing relationship with Christ. They did this by targeting un-churched students and inviting them to weekly meetings usually held in homes or some other neutral building. Each person on staff worked with one or two schools in the area where they also developed relationships with teachers, administrators and parents.

By the end of my time there, I was walking out the door with an application in my hand. Not only could I use the skills I learned in getting my education degree, I could also spend my time studying the Bible and preparing lessons geared toward drawing students closer to Jesus! The Lord was answering my heart's desire.

One detail that was mentioned up front was that each staff member was responsible for raising support, similar to a missionary. I was both excited and nervous about this prospect. After completing the application process, I was hired to work with two county schools. My salary would be a whopping $17,500 my first year which wasn't too much less than a first year teacher would make. Before I could actually begin, I had to have at least 50% raised in donations or monthly pledges. Between our church and several generous families, I was able to begin by March of 1999.

Youth For Christ had a policy where at the end of a staff person's first year, any amount received above their salary would be split 50/50. Half would go into the YFC general fund and half would be given to the staff person in the form of a check. "Cool!" I thought, not really thinking I would see anything extra.

Over the course of that first year, I found myself immersed in building relationships, planning weekly meetings, learning organization skills and just hanging out with teenagers. Most of my training was on the fly. Due to trainings and trips with students, Shelley and I were apart for a total of nearly two months in our first year of marriage. It's not something I recommend but the Lord was faithful to help us weather through that time.

As I mentioned in the beginning, we began our marriage with a hefty amount of school loans. Our goal was to pay our debt as quickly as possible. To do this, we had to live very simply. Our first apartment was a one bedroom, one bath unit within a tri-plex house. Our monthly rent ranged from $375-425 in the four years we lived there which was cheap, even for that time.

We also made a decision to try living on my meager $17,500 salary which translates to around $1,450/month. From the day we were married, we also dedicated ourselves to tithing on all our income. Time and time again, we experienced the Lord's blessing as we were faithful to give. Without a doubt, we saw the life of our cars and appliances extended. One of our cars had no business lasting as long as it did considering the wear and tear we put it through.

When the time came to file taxes for the first time as a married couple, we were excited to learn that we'd be receiving a refund of nearly $2,000. This was due to the fact that I was a student for most of 1998 and Shelley only had 6 months of Physical Therapy income. Unfortunately, we didn't have this refund the second time we filed taxes. Imagine our shock when we realized we were going to owe nearly $2,500 this time around! Ouch!

We had no savings since we were throwing every last penny into paying off those school loans. How would we pay? It was only weeks before this bomb was dropped in our laps that we sensed the Lord asking us to increase the amount we were giving. Did we hear you correctly Lord? Perhaps you meant for us to decrease our giving for a couple months? "Trust me, I know what I'm doing", said the Lord.

A couple weeks later I was sitting in my office when our Director, Paul, knocked on my door. "If you have a few minutes, I'd like to see you in my office", he said. "Did I do something wrong?" I thought to myself. Upon entering his office, I also noticed our Ministry Coordinator, Jim, sitting down. This definitely made me wonder what I did wrong. "Have a seat", they said. "Do you have any idea what this is about?" Jim asked. "Uhh...no," I responded. "It's time for your one year evaluation." This set my mind at ease as I realized I had nothing to worry about.

The three of us talked for about twenty minutes before Paul brought up the financial side of things. "You might recall our policy of writing a check for half the amount that you receive into your account above and beyond your salary?" To be honest, I had completely forgotten about this detail. He handed me an envelope and they both shook my hand. "Congratulations on making it through your first year," they said. "We're happy to have you on the YFC team."

Upon returning to my office, I slowly opened the envelope to see what it contained. Would it be $50? $100? I had no guess. As I pulled out the check and saw the amount, I was speechless. Three-thousand dollars! Are you kidding me? My eyes filled with tears as I recalled the Lord's words.

"Trust me, I know what I'm doing"

Not only did the Lord provide the amount we owed Uncle Sam in taxes, but He threw in an extra $500 for good measure. What an incredible lesson we learned that day early in our marriage. Our Heavenly Father longs to bless his children in ways we can't comprehend. Even when we can't see through our circumstances, we can trust the Lord to meet our needs.

Let's just say our faith was increased that day!

Day #2

Today God reminded me of a small binder that I started years ago with scriptures and quotes on different topics. My prayer partner at the time mentioned the idea and showed me hers. She said that she keeps her notebook handy and when she is struggling in one of the areas she listed, she will read through the scriptures over and over allowing God to renew her mind with His truth in that particular area.

I loved the idea and decided to start my own.

Believe me, mine is nothing fancy! It is simply a small binder that can hold 3.5 x 5 inch notecards. I even made homemade dividers by simply folding over a piece of scotch tape and writing the topic on it in pen.

I was so glad that I found this little binder today because it contains a quote that I wanted to share with you. Here it is…

"Faith came singing into my room, and other guests took flight. Grief, anxiety, fear and gloom, sped out into the night. I wondered that such peace could be, but faith said gently, 'Don't you see that they can never live with me?'"
~Elizabeth Cheney

Basically what she is saying in this quote is that faith and worry cannot co-exist. We will either have one or the other.

However, in many Christian circles worry is one of the greatest strongholds in our lives. Why? Well, I think one reason is that we rationalize worry (at least I know that I do) by saying we are "concerned" or have a "heavy burden" for someone. But, if we are really honest to ourselves, many times that "concern" turns to worry so easily.

And worry is a sin.

There. I said it.

Worry is a sin because we are taking our eyes off of Christ and His ability to handle a situation. And when we do this, we are no longer able to live a life of faith.

So, which will it be? Faith or doubt? Trust or worry?

2 Corinthians 5:7 says, *"For we walk by faith, not by sight."* (NKJV)

The Faith Challenge:

➤ Take a moment to say a prayer to God or write it out in your journal. Confess any sin (i.e. doubt, worry, fear, etc.) to God and be as specific as you can. Then, ask God to forgive you and help you to truly repent and turn from your sin. Ask for an empowerment of the Holy Spirit to fill you each day with faith and trust in God.

Then, anytime you slip back into worry and doubt again, simply bring it to God. Confess your sin again to Him and ask His forgiveness and empowerment to change. Deep habits take time to change, so realize that this may be a minute by minute process at first.

I encourage you to say this prayer from your heart. But if you want, you can use the following prayer I have written out below.

Lord, I come to You now admitting that I have allowed other things to take root in my mind and heart. I confess my worry, doubt and fear to You especially in regards to _____ (insert the things that you struggle with the most here). I realize that worry is a sin and that I cannot move forward in my desire for faith until I confess it to you as I am doing now. I ask You to forgive me and help me to repent and turn from my sin. I want my focus to be on You, not on my circumstances. Empower me through the Holy Spirit to change. Fill me with Your faith and a greater trust in You. I know that this journey will take time but I thank You for your grace and patience with me as I seek more of You in this *21 Days of Faith Challenge*. I love You Lord. In Jesus powerful name I pray, Amen.

Prayer of Faith: Abraham's Move

Lord, there are so many uncertainties in life, twists and turns on this journey of faith with You. Sometimes it is difficult to know what step to take next. I am thankful I can depend on You. You never change and are the same yesterday, today and forever.

When You asked Abraham to leave his home, You didn't tell him where he was going. It must have been difficult for him to leave his comfort zone and his family. However, he put his faith in You and took that first step of faith into the unknown. And You blessed him in many ways.

Lord, help me to be willing to step out in faith when You ask me. Help me to trust the unknown to You. You know the way and You will lead me one step at a time to my destination as I put my full trust in You. Thank you for leading me down the path that I should go today. Amen.

"Jesus Christ is the same yesterday and today and forever."
~ Hebrews 13:8 (ESV)

"Now the Lord said to Abram, 'Go from your country and your kindred and your father's house to the land that I will show you. And I will make of you a great nation, and I will bless you and make your name great, so that you will be a blessing. I will bless those who bless you, and him who dishonors you I will curse, and in you all the families of the earth shall be blessed.' So Abram went, as the Lord had told him, and Lot went with him. Abram was seventy-five years old when he departed from Haran."
~Genesis 12:1-4 (ESV)

"By faith Abraham obeyed when he was called to go out to the place which he would receive as an inheritance. And he went out, not knowing where he was going. By faith he dwelt in the land of promise as in a foreign country, dwelling in tents with Isaac and Jacob, the heirs with him of the same promise; for he waited for the city which has foundations, whose builder and maker is God."
~ Hebrews 11:8-10 (NKJV)

Story of Faith:
Faith of a Child

Mikayla Kayne

When the recession kicked off, it hit our blue collar town hard. Our business was failing, and we were in the process of losing our home and car. We had been struggling for over two years, sometimes living on thirty dollars a week and the kindness of others. We were learning what "living on faith" really means, and God was providing for us very much like he provided for the Israelites in the desert - just the basics, just enough, and just in time.

When our oldest son was eight, he had been dealing with our family's financial drought with amazing patience for a few years, but one Saturday morning he was especially discouraged. There was no food in the house, and he knew we had no money. As he sat quietly with his morning cartoons, letting us sleep, he prayed a simple prayer that somehow God would let him have breakfast.

As he told us later, it was only a few minutes before there was a knock at the door. Now, normally, he would have awoken us to answer it, but he peeked out and saw that it was one of our former business clients carrying a big box. My son opened the door and the man sat the box down and left without asking to see us. Inside that box was a gallon of milk, cans of spaghetti-o's, peanut butter and jelly, macaroni and cheese boxes, hot dogs and buns, juice, a loaf of bread, and a big box of Kids Crunch cereal. It was a box of kid food!

Our sweet boy was so hungry that he dug right in to the cereal and milk without a word. He put some of the groceries away and spent the rest of his morning basking in his answered prayer, and God's love that surrounded him in that moment.

When my husband and I got up, we found him sitting on the coffee table with his arm resting in the box and eyes glazed over, not really watching the infomercial that had replaced his shows. When we took it all in, we were overwhelmed not only at our friend's generosity, but at how specifically every item in that box was hand-picked to minister to our son. We knew then that our hardship was serving a greater purpose, to teach him to trust God in a deep and personal way that most American kids never have to do.

That immediate answer to an honest prayer of need cemented my son's faith, and to this day he remembers how tangibly God can show up when we need Him. It's important to teach our kids to pray, and that they know God cares about every detail of their lives. He is always paying attention, and sometimes He answers their prayers in amazing ways so that they have their very own testimony of God's faithfulness to hold onto for a lifetime.

"Therefore I say to you, do not worry about your life, what you will eat or what you will drink; nor about your body, what you will put on. Is not life more than food and the body more than clothing? Look at the birds of the air, for they neither sow nor reap nor gather into barns; yet your heavenly Father feeds them. Are you not of more value than they?"
~ Matthew 6:25-26 (NKJV)

Day #3

There are a lot of things in life that can cause worry and keep us from truly living a life of faith. And it may look different for each one of us. I know one area that triggers worry for me is uncertainty: not knowing what is going to happen or what the future holds. Another big area of worry for me this past year has been finances. For you it may be a relationship in your life or your job. The bottom line? There are a lot of things in life that can trigger worry within us.

I was reading something one day that gave a powerful illustration of what worry can be like. It caught my attention and I now want to share it with you. Here's the illustration: worry is like holding a hand grenade where the pin has already been pulled. Within time, it is going to go off. Therefore, you have two choices.

#1: You can hold on to it and allow it to damage you

Or

#2: You can throw it away

If you throw it away into the direction of other people, it can hurt them and damage them. However, you can also choose to throw it as far away from you and anyone else as possible so that no one gets hurt.

Now, if you were really holding on to a hand grenade where the pin was pulled and you knew it was going to go off in mere seconds, you would get rid of it. You would throw it away. You would get it as far away from you and anyone else as you could to avoid hurting yourself or anyone else.

However, instead, so many times in life we hold on to our worry. We allow it to fester, go off, and cause damage to ourselves or to other people. What a powerful picture that is for us as we embark on this "*21 Days of Faith Challenge.*"

So, if we truly want to live a life of faith, what should we do when the worry comes?

I Peter 5:7 gives us the answer. *"Cast all your anxiety on Him because He cares for you."* (NIV)

Jesus wants to take on our worry and anxiety. He is there. He can handle it. He can detonate our "bomb" of worry. He knows what to do with it and He is the One who can handle it. It is time to cast our worries on Him.

"The beginning of anxiety is the end of faith, and the beginning of true faith is the end of anxiety." ~ George Muller

The Faith Challenge:

➢ Do you have any worry or anxiety that you need to let go of? Are you going to hold onto it until it hurts you or those around you, or will you cast it upon Christ? I encourage you to let go of your worry and cast it upon Him because He cares for you.

➢ Go through the next 24 hours and take notice of your thoughts. When you identify worry, visualize yourself casting that worry (that circumstance or person, etc.) upon Christ.

What I do is to actually imagine my worry as a heavy backpack that I take off my shoulders and place in Jesus' hands. I then allow my shoulders to relax as I am no longer the one carrying that worry around but I am trusting it to Jesus and asking Him to handle it.

➢ Instead of worrying, pray. Then, affirm your trust in God to lead, guide and direct your steps. Sometimes all you need to say is "I trust you Jesus." It sounds simple, but it really is one of the first steps to living a life of faith.

Prayer of Faith:
Abraham's Son

Lord, thank you for all of Your promises to me in the Bible. Your Word is like a big treasure chest of promises from You. But I admit that sometimes it is hard for me to believe these promises are truly meant for me. Help me to overcome my unbelief and have faith in what You have promised me.

When you promised Abraham that he would be the father of many nations, he believed you. I am so thankful that being a person of faith does not equal perfection. Even when we fail You, You never fail us. And even though Abraham was not perfect in his journey of faith, Your Word says that he did not waver through unbelief regarding Your promise of having a son. And he and Sarah did have a son, Isaac, in their old age.

Strengthen my faith today where I am weak. Help me to believe Your promises for me and to live according to Your Word, not my feelings. I love you so much. Thank you for continuing to work in my life. Amen.

"If we are faithless, He remains faithful - for He cannot deny Himself."

~ 2 Timothy 2:13 (ESV)

"This is my covenant with you: I will make you the father of a multitude of nations! What's more, I am changing your name. It will no longer be Abram. Instead, you will be called Abraham, for you will be the father of many nations. I will make you extremely fruitful. Your descendants will become many nations, and kings will be among them!

~ Genesis 17:4-6 (NLT)

"Without weakening in his faith, he (Abraham) faced the fact that his body was as good as dead—since he was about a hundred years old—and that Sarah's womb was also dead. Yet he did not waver through unbelief regarding the promise of God, but was strengthened in his faith and gave glory to God, being fully persuaded that God had power to do what he had promised. This is why 'it was credited to him as righteousness.'"

~ Romans 4:19-22 (NIV)

Story of Faith:
A Journey to Doubtless Faith
Mary L. Ball

Faith, such a simple word, but those five letters together conjure all sorts of meanings. As humans we have faith in lots of things. When we start our vehicle, we are confident that it will purr to life. Each day we flick a switch on the wall and believe that the lights will shine a glow brightening the room.

That's worldly assurance, something we all have. Putting your trust in God is the test of a true faith.

25

I remember back when I was seeking to become a published writer. I inscribe various flash stories and still produce weekly Christian articles; nevertheless, writing a fiction novel stretched my creativity.

Carving out an inspirational novel was a heart's desire. I wanted to use my writing, not only to reaffirm God's word, but to generate fictional characters that have everyday problems and overcome situations by the grace and mercy of Jesus Christ.

From the beginning to end, the process included four re-writes and lots of critiques. As with any debut author, doubts entered into my mind. I stood resilient in the Lord, replacing those uncertainties with faith.

For the next year, I held on to several verses from my King James Bible. The process of fine-tuning my manuscript crept on and rejection emails poured in from publishers.

As I would hit the delete button on my laptop and toss the notes in the trash, I voiced faith that a contract was on its way. I quoted one of my favorite stanzas from the book of Mark, placing emphasis on the words, "shall not doubt." The scripture is in chapter eleven, verse twenty-three.

"For verily I say unto you, That whosoever shall say unto this mountain, Be thou removed, and be thou cast into the sea; and shall not doubt in his heart, but shall believe that those things which he saith shall come to pass; he shall have whatsoever he saith." (KJV)

Furthermore, I believe there's power in the words we speak. In church, I declared to the congregation, testifying that I would become a published author.

"Death and life are in the power of the tongue: and they that love it shall eat the fruit thereof."
~ Proverbs 18:21 (KJV)

To me, speaking out a confirmation of the promises God offers is also a show of faith. The one important thing about having faith isn't standing in the belief of God's word for a while; it's having confidence in the assurances of the Lord's promises for the long haul. Faith must withstand time. It can't be a here today and gone tomorrow kind of trust.

The road to becoming a published author was long. It took a year and a half. Lots of re-writes and submitting to about fifty publishers.

Finally, the day came that I was offered a contract from a publisher willing to take a chance with a new author. I remember it was just before Christmas, and I fondly told my friends that even though it was Jesus' birthday I had received a Christmas present from Him.

I think back to those days and realize that when I faced my "mountain" of not being published, I took one day at a time and believed what is to come. Thank goodness, I had the strength not to waver.

In all our lives, we need to have a permanent belief that God can cause a change. Steadfast confidence is the key component to faith coming alive. What would have happened if I gave in to insecurities? For me, losing faith wasn't an option. I had a goal even though the world had objections. I know God has the final say, not men.

God wants good things for his children. If we abide in him, then he'll be true to us, so long as we aren't holding on to something that can be harmful to our growth as a follower of

Christ. Maybe we don't get the results we want every time, but God's still in control. The Lord knows what's best for all of us.

We must hold on to our faith regardless of the mountain we perceive. Be certain, without a doubt; never give in to what the world says about you or the accomplishments you desire. Turn on the switch of faith by reading God's word and believe you can receive.

Day #4

This past 18 months of our lives has been marked with one word...transition. I officially resigned my job as a Physical Therapist at the end of July 2011. Then we moved into a small Toyota RV and lived in 125 square feet of space for 3.5 months...full time. We downsized our earthly belongings and everything we needed fit in either our small RV or our small car.

It was our dream to travel and speak across the country in a RV. However, things didn't work out as we thought or planned. We ended up selling the RV and moving to Colorado instead.

And I was confused.

I had resigned my job as a P.T. to travel and minister and speak full-time with CJ and then...nothing. Silence. It felt like God was silent.

Have You Ever Experienced a Time When God Seemed Distant or Silent in Your Life?

I think we all experience moments when God seems distant or silent in our lives.

During this current season of transition in my life, it has often felt like I can't see clearly what the next steps will be. I have a strong relationship with Jesus and have had seasons where I could sense His voice and leading clearly in my life.

The picture I get of this season of life is of a fog that has descended over me. I cannot see anything except what is right in front of me...the present moment. I don't know where we will be going and what we will be doing. I don't know how we will pay the bills (although God has provided and we have been able to pay every one of them thus far).

And I Won't Lie to You...It Has Been Hard. Really Hard.

I like to be in control and have a plan. It is difficult to walk by faith. I never realized how much I depended on my regular paycheck from the hospital until we did not have it. I realize now that I was depending more on that steady paycheck than I was on God.

I am not saying that everyone needs to quit their jobs and venture out in faith to learn these lessons. This is simply the path that we have been on these last few months.

And as hard as it has been, it has also been good.

There was a root of self-sufficiency in me that is slowly being uprooted. I am still in the process, but God is teaching me to fully rely on Him and not on my own efforts. He is proving Himself to me over and over as He provides for us something that I never could.

An Illustration of Faith

I woke up to a rainy day just weeks after moving to Colorado and saw something amazing when I looked out our front window. Normally we can see Pikes Peak VERY clearly from our front window. But, that day...nothing. Literally. I could not see the mountain AT ALL. It was almost as if it was not there anymore.

Instantly, God spoke to my heart.

Just because I couldn't see Pikes Peak that morning, didn't mean it was no longer there. The mountain was still there. I know it was because I have seen it so many times in that very same place. It was just that the clouds of that particular day kept the mountain hidden from me.

And So it is With God Sometimes as Well.

There are those bright sunny days where everything seems to be going my way and I can sense God's presence and His voice leading and guiding me so clearly. Then there are other days that seem cloudy and gray, where God seems distant and silent in my life.

It doesn't mean that God isn't there. God is still there. He has proven Himself to me over and over again. It's just that the "clouds" of the day have descended over me at the moment.

And so in those moments when God seems distant or silent, it comes down to trust. Trusting that He's still there, just like I trust Pikes Peak to still be there even though I can't see it clearly from my window.

What does it mean to trust? Well, here's a definition from the dictionary:

Trust (noun)

1. reliance on the integrity, strength, ability, surety, etc., of a person or thing; confidence.

2. confident expectation of something; hope.

3. confidence in the certainty of future payment for property or goods received; credit: to sell merchandise on trust.

4. a person on whom or thing on which one relies: God is my trust.

5. the condition of one to whom something has been entrusted.

And so, when I am in the midst of the fog, I trust that God is with me.

"Never doubt in the dark what God told you in the light."
~ Raymond Edman

"Never be afraid to trust an unknown future to a known God."
~ Corrie ten Boom

"Trust in the Lord with all your heart and lean not on your own understanding; in all your ways submit to him, and he will make your paths straight."
~ Proverbs 3:5-6 (NIV)

The Faith Challenge:

➤ Can you relate to feeling distant to God? Journal about a time when God seemed distant in your life or share it with a friend.

➤ Then, choose to trust God today. Even if you are in the middle of a fog and cannot see Him or hear Him clearly, know that He is still there. Affirm your trust in Him by saying a simple prayer, *"I trust You, Jesus, even when I cannot see or understand."*

Prayer of Faith:
Abraham's Sacrifice

Lord, living a life of faith is not always easy. Sometimes it requires a sacrifice of my time, money and/or relationships. If You ask me to give something up, it is for a purpose. Also, help me to realize that when You ask me to sacrifice something, it is for my good. You want to be first in my life, but so often I have put other idols before You. Please forgive me. I specifically confess that I often put _____ (fill in the blank) before You. Please forgive me and help me to love You with ALL my heart, soul, mind and strength.

When you asked Abraham to sacrifice his son, the son that was going to fulfill Your promise to him, he obeyed. He believed that You could raise Isaac up from the dead in order to still fulfill Your promise. Wow...what faith! You tested Abraham and he showed by his obedience that You were first in his heart...not his son. And you stopped him from harming Isaac and provided a ram for the offering instead.

Thank you, Lord, for this vivid example of faith. Strengthen my faith in You today and may I continue to put You first in my life above anyone or anything else. In Jesus' name I pray, Amen.

"And one of the scribes came up and heard them disputing with one another, and seeing that he answered them well, asked him, 'Which commandment is the most important of all?' Jesus answered, 'The most important is, 'Hear, O Israel: The Lord our God, the Lord is one. And you shall love the Lord your God with all your heart and with all your soul and with all your mind and with all your strength.'"
~ Mark 12:28-30 (ESV)

"Now it came to pass after these things that God tested Abraham, and said to him, 'Abraham!' And he said, 'Here I am.' Then He said, 'Take now your son, your only son Isaac, whom you love, and go to the land of Moriah, and offer him there as a burnt offering on one of the mountains of which I shall tell you.'"

~ Genesis 22:1-2 (NKJV)

"And He said, 'Do not lay your hand on the lad, or do anything to him; for now I know that you fear God, since you have not withheld your son, your only son, from Me.' Then Abraham lifted his eyes and looked, and there behind him was a ram caught in a thicket by its horns. So Abraham went and took the ram, and offered it up for a burnt offering instead of his son. And Abraham called the name of the place, The-Lord-Will-Provide; as it is said to this day, 'In the Mount of the Lord it shall be provided.'"

~ Genesis 22:12-14 (NKJV)

"By faith Abraham, when he was tested, offered up Isaac, and he who had received the promises offered up his only begotten son, of whom it was said, 'In Isaac your seed shall be called,' concluding that God was able to raise him up, even from the dead, from which he also received him in a figurative sense."

~ Hebrews 11:17-19 (NKJV)

Also read: Entire chapter of Genesis 22

Story of Faith:
The Testament of Faith

Nishoni Harvey

"The beginning of anxiety is the end of faith, and the beginning of true faith is the end of anxiety."
~ George Mueller

My dad was out of work due to an extensive knee surgery and ended up losing his job due to the recovery time. Times were tough, and money was hard to come by. They prayed fervently for God to provide another job for my father. Days turned into months and God had not yet seen fit to answer their prayers. They held to their faith in God and trusted in His promise that He would supply all their needs according to His riches in Glory by Christ Jesus. Still, my parents watched helplessly as the money in the bank and the food in the pantry dwindled. Soon, there was no food left in the house.

With two small children to feed, they set off for the river one day in hopes of catching enough fish for dinner. After many fruitless hours and with heavy hearts and dashed hopes, they started the short trek back home. They knew God wouldn't let them down. He had promised that He would provide, but all they had caught were two small brim. They carried them home, praying that it would be enough to satisfy my sister and me.

Upon returning home, they couldn't believe their eyes! The whole porch was covered with bags and bags of groceries! They wondered where the food had come from and how anyone knew they were in need. They had not told anyone, including family, about their financial situation. They had told no one, that is, except for God.

Attached to one of the bags was a tag that simply read, "From the three of us". My parents called everyone they could think of. No one would admit to leaving any packages on our stoop. Because God had rewarded their faith and provided where no one else could, we simply hold to the knowledge that it was a blessing and gift from God. We hold to our belief that "the three of us" who signed the tag on the bag was God the Father, God the Son, and God the Holy Spirit. What else can we think?

To this day, twenty-seven years later, we have never learned who our angels were, but we did learn a few new things. God always provides for His children. When the day seems dark and there seems to be no way out, look up. Have faith. Not only does God always have the answer, but God always is the answer.

In the years since, I've faced many trying times. My faith has been tested and stretched many times over, but God always reminds me of this story. The faith my earthly father held in my Heavenly Father still gives me reason to trust to this day. The way God rewarded that faith has always been a testament to me of how faith in God's promises will always pull me through, making me stronger in the end.

"I have been young, and now am old; yet have I not seen the righteous forsaken, nor his seed begging bread."
~ Psalm 37:25 (KJV)

Day #5

Years ago, I received a personalized quote in a picture frame. Even as we were downsizing from our house to a small RV, I decided to keep it. And I am glad I did. God is using it during this season of my life to speak to me.

It says, *"Shelley, Trust Me. I have everything under control. ~ Jesus"*

Many times we need tangible reminders like this to remind us that we can trust Jesus with the circumstances of our lives. Even when we cannot see all the details, He has everything under control.

"When a train goes through a tunnel and it gets dark, you don't throw away the ticket and jump off. You sit still and trust the engineer."

~ Corrie ten Boom

"May the God of hope fill you with all joy and peace as you trust in him, so that you may overflow with hope by the power of the Holy Spirit."

~ Romans 15:13 (NIV)

The Faith Challenge:

➢ Write out this following quote and personalize it with your name. Then, post it somewhere you will see it every day.

_____ (insert your name),

Trust Me. I have everything under control.

~ Jesus

Prayer of Faith:
David and Goliath

Lord, some days my circumstances threaten to overwhelm me. It is on those days when I am tempted to worry and feel defeated. However, I know that I am never alone. You are always with me and are my strength and my provider. Help me to remember to set my mind on You and not on my circumstances.

David literally faced a giant in battle…Goliath. All the odds were against him, but he chose to trust in You. David learned to keep his eyes fixed on You and not on his circumstances. And You gave him a great victory.

Empower me to have faith like David today. A faith that trusts in Your power and not my own. A faith that knows that You are greater than any "giants" I face today. My story may end differently than David's did, but I choose to trust my circumstances to You today. Thank you for the victory You will grant me. In Jesus' name I pray, Amen.

"Set your minds on things that are above, not on things that are on earth."

~ Colossians 3:2 (ESV)

"David said to the Philistine, 'You come against me with sword and spear and javelin, but I come against you in the name of the Lord Almighty, the God of the armies of Israel, whom you have defied. This day the Lord will deliver you into my hands, and I'll strike you down and cut off your head. This very day I will give the carcasses of the Philistine army to the birds and the wild animals, and the whole world will know that there is a God in Israel. All those gathered here will know that it is not by sword or spear that the Lord saves; for the battle is the Lord's, and he will give all of you into our hands.'"

~ I Samuel 17:45-47 (NIV)

Also read: Entire chapter of I Samuel 17

Story of Faith:
A Broken Finger
Ruth Kyser

I never thought I'd be thankful for a broken finger.

A number of years ago I was having an extremely difficult time in my job. I was going through a period of deep discouragement and depression, stuck in a career I'd fallen into which wasn't necessarily of my choosing. I eventually made the decision to mail out resumes and apply for some other jobs in the hopes that something better would come along. I could hardly wait!

Months went by and nothing seemed to happen and that just made me more upset with my job. Looking back on it now, I realize I was making myself absolutely miserable. A part of me must have realized this because I made the commitment to spend more time in prayer and Bible reading, hoping beyond hope to discover God's will. Did He want me to leave my current job and start a new career, or did He want me to stay where I was? And if He wanted me to stay, why was I so miserable?

I admit it, I'm human. When I didn't get a firm answer from God, I took it upon myself to make the decision without waiting for Him. I know – bad move! I decided if a job opportunity came along that was realistic, I was taking it. Shortly after that, I applied for a job at a school and believed after the first interview went well that it was supposed to be mine.

Then God spoke. Oh, I didn't hear His voice, but nonetheless, He spoke.

A misstep and the resulting tumble where my face met a concrete sidewalk resulted in a broken finger. There was little chance of me getting this new job now. Who was going to hire me with a splint on my finger? I couldn't type or write with that hand.

I wasn't very happy with God right then. Not only was I stuck in the job I was trying to get away from, but I was also going to have to do the job one-handed, and my broken finger hurt! It was a humbling experience for someone as independent as I am. Everything took me longer to accomplish. However, as I was forced to slow down, I began to look at it all differently – particularly my job. It was a good-paying job and instead of finding fault with it, I decided to be thankful for it – and for my bosses who appreciated my work (even my one-handed work). Suddenly, my attitude changed and consequently, so did my outlook on life.

I'd been looking for a sign from God all this time about what to do with my job. This is what I discovered: He didn't want me to change my job. He wanted me to change my attitude. When I finally did that, my whole outlook changed.

My faith in my Heavenly Father was restored. As always, He knew what was best for me even though I hadn't wanted to listen to Him. A broken finger had shown me He had me right where I was supposed to be. In hindsight I can tell you without a doubt that not leaving my job was for the best. Because of budget cuts, the position I was vying for at the school turned out to be temporary. If I had accepted that job, I would have soon been out of work.

During this time one of my favorite verses became Romans 8:28. I'd read it a hundred times, but as we so often do, I had never applied the words of the verse to my own life.

"And we know that all things work together for good to them that love God, to them who are the called according to his purpose." (KJV)

Do I believe God caused me to fall and break my finger? I don't believe He did, although He did take a bad event in my life and turned it into something for my good.

And for that broken finger, I will be forever thankful.

Day #6

What does it look like to trust God? Many times it is easy to talk about faith and trust, but it is hard to visualize how it plays out in our everyday lives. Right before I was to resign my job and launch into full time ministry with CJ, God graciously gave me a picture of what faith looks like. A speaker at a conference demonstrated this illustration so clearly to me.

The speaker stood on the stage and described a season in his family's life when God asked them to step out in faith. He then asked for a volunteer to come up on the stage, directed them to stand up on a table, and then blindfolded them. He turned them around so the volunteer's back was facing the audience.

As he continued to tell his story of trusting God, he quietly began to pull people out of the audience and line them up behind the volunteer. He shared how difficult it was to trust God because he could not see how it would all work out. But, unbeknownst to the speaker, God had a plan developing behind the scenes.

After he lined up around 5-6 people on each side in two parallel lines facing each other, he had them join arms with the person across from them to form a "safety net" behind the volunteer standing on the table. Now remember, all of this was happening quietly and without the knowledge of the volunteer who had been blindfolded.

Finally, the speaker asked the volunteer if he trusted him. The speaker said he had everything under control and was trustworthy. He then asked the volunteer to fall back into a trust fall. However, the volunteer had no idea that there were 10-12 strong and capable people behind him ready to catch him when he fell.

And instantly God spoke to my heart.

Just because I could not see how this next phase of our lives was going to work out, I could trust Him. He was behind the scenes working everything out and providing that "safety net" for CJ and I.

And you know what?

When I reflect back upon the past 18 months of our lives, I can see how we have lived out this illustration. In many ways, it felt like God asked us to stand on a cliff blindfolded and jump off. Finances have been very tight, but we always had what we needed. As my husband has so often reminded me over these last months, there has not been one bill we couldn't pay. We have had food and shelter. God has provided...and sometimes in the most unexpected ways, through means I could never have dreamed, planned or figured out.

I will admit that I have tears in my eyes as I type this out today. Why? Well, even though God has seemed silent during this season of my life, looking back I realize that He was providing for us all along. He has been active in our lives - caring for us in ways I did not, or could not, see at the time.

When we live a life of faith, we may feel like we are walking through our circumstances blindfolded. However, our God sees everything and is able to provide in ways that we cannot even imagine. That is, if we will trust Him.

"God will never, never, never let us down if we have faith and put our trust in Him. He will always look after us. So we must cleave to Jesus. Our whole life must simply be woven into Jesus."

~ Mother Teresa

"Often I have heard people say, 'How good God is! We prayed that it would not rain for our church picnic, and look at the lovely weather!' Yes, God is good when He sends good weather. But God was also good when He allowed my sister, Betsie, to starve to death before my eyes in a German concentration camp. I remember one occasion when I was very discouraged there. Everything around us was dark, and there was darkness in my heart. I remember telling Betsie that I thought God had forgotten us. 'No, Corrie,' said Betsie, 'He has not forgotten us. Remember His Word: For as the heavens are high above the earth, so great is His steadfast love toward those who fear Him.' Corrie concludes, 'There is an ocean of God's love available - there is plenty for everyone. May God grant you never to doubt that victorious love - whatever the circumstances.'"

~ Corrie ten Boom

"Though He slay me, yet will I trust Him."

~ Job 13:15 (NKJV)

The Faith Challenge:

> ➢ It is easy to trust God in the good times, but more difficult to trust Him during the hard times. In prayer, ask God to help you trust Him regardless of your circumstances.

Prayer of Faith:
Joshua and Caleb

Thank you, Lord, for all that You have given me. I am truly blessed. And yet sometimes I listen to the lies of the enemy, Satan, who causes doubt and fear to enter my mind and heart. Help me to recognize the lies of the enemy and replace them with Your Truth.

Joshua and Caleb were among the spies who went into the land that God promised to them. It was an amazing land flowing with milk and honey. However, all of the spies except for two, Joshua and Caleb, allowed their fear of the giants in the land to keep them from enjoying the blessing You had for them. Joshua and Caleb put their trust in You and had faith that You would bring them into the land. And they ended up being the only Israelites from their generation to enter the Promised Land years later.

Lord, thank You that You have not given us a spirit of fear, but of love and self-control. Your love, perfect love, drives out fear. Therefore, I ask You to remove any fear in my heart and mind today and replace it with Your peace. Thank You for Your presence with me today. Amen.

"But Joshua the son of Nun and Caleb the son of Jephunneh, who were among those who had spied out the land, tore their clothes; and they spoke to all the congregation of the children of Israel, saying: 'The land we passed through to spy out is an exceedingly good land. If the Lord delights in us, then He will bring us into this land and give it to us, 'a land which flows with milk and honey.' Only do not rebel against the Lord, nor fear the people of the land, for they are our bread; their

*protection has departed from them, and the Lord is with us.
Do not fear them.'"*

~ Numbers 14:6-9 (NKJV)

*"'Of all those I rescued from Egypt, no one who is twenty
years old or older will ever see the land I swore to give to
Abraham, Isaac, and Jacob, for they have not obeyed me
wholeheartedly. The only exceptions are Caleb son of
Jephunneh the Kenizzite and Joshua son of Nun, for they have
wholeheartedly followed the Lord.'"*

~ Numbers 32:11-12 (NLT)

*"For God gave us a spirit not of fear but of power and love
and self-control."*

~ 2 Timothy 1:7 (ESV)

*"There is no fear in love, but perfect love casts out fear. For
fear has to do with punishment, and whoever fears has not
been perfected in love."*

~1 John 4:18 (ESV)

Also read: Numbers 13-14

Story of Faith:
Stepping Out of My Comfort Zone
Krystal Kuehn

"I could never do that," I thought, as I listened to the music
during the Sunday morning service. I thought it was
courageous of Pat to volunteer to play the piano when the
church had no one else. She hadn't played for very long, and
she struggled through most of the songs. Then I couldn't help
but think of how I had played the guitar and sang for many
years; and yet, I was reluctant to volunteer. "When I feel

ready," is what I would always say to myself. And now here was someone who did not wait to be "ready" or "good enough." She decided to serve God with her limited abilities. That is not just courageous; it is humbling. It takes humility and faith to be willing to fail and be less than perfect. It made me wonder if I was more concerned with what people thought than I was with giving God what I had.

The Lord was dealing with my heart concerning my attitude. James 4:10 (KJV) struck a chord in me: *"Humble yourselves in the sight of the Lord, and he shall lift you up."* Immediately my reaction was one of fear. I always associated humility with humiliation and embarrassment. "Oh please," I prayed, "Don't ask me so do something I can't do." Of course I knew that the Lord would never require that of his children. What I was actually praying was that I wouldn't be expected to do something that I didn't want to do or do something that was outside my comfort zone – something that would require me to humble myself before God and trust that He has my best interest at heart.

Over the years, I often confessed that I can do all things through Christ who gives me strength (Philippians 4:13). I didn't realize that now I needed strength to be humble. I never thought of myself as prideful. I was never out to show off or prove myself to anyone. But, as God spoke to my heart, I realized for the first time that God wanted me to be willing to sacrifice my pride to be obedient to Him. I soon had the opportunity to do just that in a way I least expected.

I prayed all week for an upcoming jazz session I was joining for the first time. I believed that God opened the door for this opportunity; so naturally, I wanted to be obedient. It was new to me and I knew it would be challenging, but I was confident that anything God had for me to do was possible with His help. It wasn't too difficult to trust and believe God as long as I felt comfortable and somewhat in control.

The jazz session turned out worse than I could have ever imagined. I didn't make it through a single song successfully. I felt like I failed miserably. I cried all the way home. "I can't do it," I told myself. It wasn't that I couldn't try real hard; learn from my mistakes, and eventually get it right. Rather, it was that I couldn't imagine being in a situation where I felt so humbled, and where my struggle and weaknesses were apparent to everyone.

As difficult as it would be, I knew I had to call my mentor who recommended me for the position. I told him that I was going to wait until I was "ready" and "good enough;" and I would try again then. He refused to let me quit. He refused to lose confidence in me. To my surprise, I couldn't talk my way out of it. He refuted my every argument until I felt completely drained and out of excuses. Hesitantly, I agreed to stay in the band.

Every time I thought about facing the band again, I felt a dreadful, sick feeling inside. It would have been so much easier to stay "comfortable." But deep inside I knew that if I was to trust God and walk by faith, I would have to grow and change; and there is no way of getting around the discomfort. I would have to walk by faith if I was going to be obedient. I would have to believe God in a way I never had before.

Then as I pondered the beauty of God's nature, I realized that He wants my ultimate best. He believes in me, and He doesn't give up on me no matter where I am at in my life. He doesn't want me to quit when I get uncomfortable. There is something He wants to do in me – something greater than I can imagine or comprehend. All I must do is submit to His will, and by faith, look past the present discomfort and pain. And God will take my circumstances and use them for His glory. The experience with the jazz band turned out to be one of the most rewarding and successful musical experiences I ever had. I not only grew in my faith, I grew as a musician. It prepared me for upcoming orchestral projects and much more. God's way is always the best if we would only believe!

I wondered about all the opportunities where I may have missed God by my lack of faith, times He wanted me to simply believe and trust Him to work out His plan for my life. It is so much easier to excuse ourselves, justify our complacency, or postpone what God would have us to do now to a time when we feel "ready." Unfortunately, that time seldom comes. The time to believe and serve the Lord is NOW. If we start with what we have, it is "good enough" for God.

Day #7:

Many times, Hebrews 11 is called the "Hall of Faith" chapter. I often think of it like the "Hall of Fame" where certain members get inducted. However, the members in God's "Hall of Faith" were chosen due to the faith they demonstrated in their lives.

Here are the names listed within this chapter:

- Abel
- Enoch
- Noah
- Abraham
- Sarah
- Isaac
- Jacob
- Joseph
- Moses
- Rahab
- Gideon
- Barak
- Samson
- Jephthah
- David
- Samuel
- And the prophets

Do you recognize any of these names? I am sure you did! However, today I encourage you to read this entire chapter to learn even more about what faith looks like. And as you do, make sure you don't miss this verse:

"But without faith it is impossible to please Him, for he who comes to God must believe that He is, and that He is a rewarder of those who diligently seek Him."
~ Hebrews 11:6 (NKJV)

Do you want to please God? If so, you must have faith! Let's keep seeking to live a life of faith that pleases Him.

"Dependence upon God makes heroes of ordinary people like you and me!"
~ Bruce Wilkinson

The Faith Challenge:

➤ Read Hebrews 11, the "Hall of Faith." Write at least 2 things in your journal that you learn about faith from this chapter.

Prayer of Faith:
Queen Esther

Lord, thank you for another day of life. You are the One who gives breath to my lungs. You also know all the days ordained for me as they have been written in Your book.

I know that You have created me for a purpose, and that purpose is to glorify You. Just as You placed Queen Esther in the King's household "for such a time as this" to save her people, You also have plans and purposes for my life. Queen Esther was willing to risk her life to come before the King on

51

behalf of the Jewish people. I ask that You empower me today with courage through Your Holy Spirit to take risks for You. I come to you with a surrendered heart, Lord. May Your will be done in my life.

I love you so much. Amen.

"Your eyes saw my unformed body; all the days ordained for me were written in Your book before one of them came to be."
~ Psalm 139:16 (NIV)

"When Esther's words were reported to Mordecai, he sent back this answer: 'Do not think that because you are in the king's house you alone of all the Jews will escape. For if you remain silent at this time, relief and deliverance for the Jews will arise from another place, but you and your father's family will perish. And who knows but that you have come to your royal position for such a time as this?' Then Esther sent this reply to Mordecai: 'Go, gather together all the Jews who are in Susa, and fast for me. Do not eat or drink for three days, night or day. I and my attendants will fast as you do. When this is done, I will go to the king, even though it is against the law. And if I perish, I perish.'"
~ Esther 4:12-16 (NIV)

"Then Esther went again before the king, falling down at his feet and begging him with tears to stop the evil plot devised by Haman the Agagite against the Jews. Again the king held out the gold scepter to Esther. So she rose and stood before him. Esther said, 'If it please the king, and if I have found favor with him, and if he thinks it is right, and if I am pleasing to him, let there be a decree that reverses the orders of Haman son of Hammedatha the Agagite, who ordered that Jews throughout all the king's provinces should be destroyed. For

how can I endure to see my people and my family slaughtered and destroyed?'

Then King Xerxes said to Queen Esther and Mordecai the Jew, 'I have given Esther the property of Haman, and he has been impaled on a pole because he tried to destroy the Jews. Now go ahead and send a message to the Jews in the king's name, telling them whatever you want, and seal it with the king's signet ring. But remember that whatever has already been written in the king's name and sealed with his signet ring can never be revoked.'"

~ Esther 8:3-8 (NLT)

Also read: Book of Esther

Story of Faith: My Story of Faith
Cliff Ball

God gave me the ability to write at a very young age, which sparked an interest in me when I was about eight after my parents bought me some novels to read. These included Robinson Crusoe, Treasure Island, Gulliver's Travels, a couple Christian-based young adult novels, and even the Little House series (my parents weren't readers, so they didn't think about the Little House series being mostly read by girls).

The Little House TV series sparked an even bigger interest in me because it had just ended. I mostly became interested in Laura's story of how she became an author and I thought I wanted to do that too. So, after spending lots of time writing (in the age before e-mail) to the various places around the country where Laura used to live to find out how she came up with what she came up with, I began to write when I was ten.

I wrote short stories here and there, submitted to various contests and magazines sporadically throughout the years, but never thought about doing anything serious with it. By the way, in my teens, I moved on from that interest in how Laura wrote, to being interested in reading and writing mostly science fiction novels (in case you're wondering).

Years later, as an adult in my 30's, my faith was tested when I was laid off from my job in October 2009. I had been praying and praying and applying for a job in a library for years, and then God finally granted me what I asked for. Unfortunately, I had moved to a new town specifically because I wanted to go to a particular church where the city happened to have a college to go to, but I slowly fell out of church once I got the job. I didn't realize this was a mistake until I'd been laid off, but I had faith that after I finished my last semester of college, which was the same year, that God would just up and grant me a new job.

That's not what happened. As a teenager, my parents had me pick a life verse, which I chose from Proverbs 3-5:6 KJV: "Trust in the Lord with all thine heart; and lean not unto thine own understanding. In all thy ways acknowledge him, and he shall direct thy paths." As an adult, I had a very hard time following this verse, because I really hadn't done any of that. I wanted to go my own way and I hardly ever gave God the acknowledgement in anything I did, whether I succeeded or failed. It would be a while before I realized that I had to rely completely on God.

At this same time, I had already published two novels thanks to the ease of the internet and being able to do it yourself, but I considered writing to be a hobby, nothing more. After being laid off, I felt God's influence and He was telling me to write Christian-based novels, but I didn't want to, and I ignored Him, because I wanted to write what I wanted to write.

Because of that attitude, I wasn't very successful as a published author. I also hadn't had very much success finding a new job, so I was incredibly discouraged, but figured that I needed to return to college to get my GPA up so that I could get a Master's in Technical Communication, and then someone would hire me. All that did was get me deeper in student loan debt, since I didn't get accepted into the MTC program at the University I was going to here in Texas. Instead of doing what God wanted me to do or even praying about it, which was write Christian-based novels, I got into deeper trouble.

In late 2011, I finally started listening to what God wanted, but it took my mom, who wasn't a writer, or a reader for that matter, but a very strong Christian, to help steer me to what God wanted me to do. God gave her an idea for a story which I kept dismissing, so she ignored me (for which I'm grateful), and wrote down an outline for the entire thing. She gave it to me around Thanksgiving, but I was still really hesitant to write the novel. My attitude was: Who reads anything Christian besides the Left Behind series? But, after Christmas, I decided I would give it a shot.

Boy was I surprised when I started writing. The story flowed out of me, to the point where I didn't want to stop writing, and I could feel God's influence as I was writing it. This felt odd to me, mostly because I hadn't really felt His presence like that since I was a child. I usually write every few days or once a week before this, but I wrote every day, sometimes more than five hours at a time, on this novel for thirty days straight.

When I was done, I felt drained of energy, but I finally felt like I did something that God had wanted me to do for a long time. Then, I published the novel, Times of Trouble, a few weeks later. I was astounded that it took off, since the doubting Thomas in me thought it would never sell, and ever since, the novel has been selling on average two a day between Amazon and Barnes & Noble. I don't know why exactly, but writing that novel helped me to see that I should have faith in God's plans for me, even though I don't know where He's taking me on this journey as a writer. I look forward to it.

Day #8:

Today I want to share a story from Mark 9:17-27 (NKJV).

"Then one of the crowd answered and said, 'Teacher, I brought You my son, who has a mute spirit. And wherever it seizes him, it throws him down; he foams at the mouth, gnashes his teeth, and becomes rigid. So I spoke to Your disciples, that they should cast it out, but they could not.'

He answered him and said, 'O faithless generation, how long shall I be with you? How long shall I bear with you? Bring him to Me.' Then they brought him to Him. And when he saw Him, immediately the spirit convulsed him, and he fell on the ground and wallowed, foaming at the mouth.

So He asked his father, 'How long has this been happening to him?'

And he said, 'From childhood. And often he has thrown him both into the fire and into the water to destroy him. But if You can do anything, have compassion on us and help us.'

Jesus said to him, 'If you can believe, all things are possible to him who believes.'

Immediately the father of the child cried out and said with tears, 'Lord, I believe; help my unbelief!'

When Jesus saw that the people came running together, He rebuked the unclean spirit, saying to it: 'Deaf and dumb spirit, I command you, come out of him and enter him no more!' Then the spirit cried out, convulsed him greatly, and came out of him. And he became as one dead, so that many said, 'He is dead.' But Jesus took him by the hand and lifted him up, and he arose."

There is so much we could discuss regarding faith in this passage. However, today I want to focus on the father's response to Jesus. The child's father said, *"Lord, I believe; help my unbelief!"*

The KJV says it this way, "And straightway the father of the child cried out, and said with tears, Lord, I believe; help thou mine unbelief."

The father cried out with tears.

From this description, the father was definitely NOT feeling complacent or lackadaisical as he responded to Jesus. Instead, he responded with passion and honesty. He was honest that he still struggled with unbelief. But with a passionate plea, he reached out and asked for Jesus' help. And Jesus responded to him by healing his son.

This is a prayer you can also use when you struggle with faith or believing God. Simply say, "Lord, I believe; help my unbelief!"

"Relying on God has to begin all over again every day as if nothing had yet been done."
                                                                    ~C.S. Lewis

The Faith Challenge:

➤ When faced with doubt and uncertainty, reach out for Jesus' help by praying the simple prayer of the child's father, *"Lord, I believe; help my unbelief!"*

Prayer of Faith:
Shadrach, Meshach & Abed-nego

Lord, there are so many things in this world that compete for my time, attention and worship. It is so easy to get caught up in worldly pursuits instead of spending time worshipping You. Please forgive me for neglecting my relationship with You. I truly do want to put You first in my life.

Empower me to take a stand in my culture like Shadrach, Meshach, and Abed-Nego did. Instead of bowing down and worshipping the golden image of Nebuchadnezzar, they took a stand for You. They declared that You were able to deliver them from the fiery furnace, but even if You did not, they would not compromise their beliefs. Wow. And You did deliver them from the furnace and rewarded them for their obedience to You.

No matter what the outcome may be, Lord, grant me a willingness to obey You. Strengthen my faith in You. Thank You for opening my eyes to Your Truth and drawing me to Yourself. I pray that I would stand strong in Your strength and not my own strength when my faith is challenged. In Jesus' name I pray, Amen.

"Then Nebuchadnezzar, in rage and fury, gave the command to bring Shadrach, Meshach, and Abed-Nego. So they brought these men before the king. Nebuchadnezzar spoke, saying to them, 'Is it true, Shadrach, Meshach, and Abed-Nego, that you do not serve my gods or worship the gold image which I have set up? Now if you are ready at the time you hear the sound of the horn, flute, harp, lyre, and psaltery, in symphony with all kinds of music, and you fall down and worship the image which I have made, good! But if you do not worship, you shall

be cast immediately into the midst of a burning fiery furnace. And who is the god who will deliver you from my hands?'

Shadrach, Meshach, and Abed-Nego answered and said to the king, 'O Nebuchadnezzar, we have no need to answer you in this matter. If that is the case, our God whom we serve is able to deliver us from the burning fiery furnace, and He will deliver us from your hand, O king. But if not, let it be known to you, O king, that we do not serve your gods, nor will we worship the gold image which you have set up.'

... 'Look!' he answered, 'I see four men loose, walking in the midst of the fire; and they are not hurt, and the form of the fourth is like the Son of God.' Then Nebuchadnezzar went near the mouth of the burning fiery furnace and spoke, saying, 'Shadrach, Meshach, and Abed-Nego, servants of the Most High God, come out, and come here.' Then Shadrach, Meshach, and Abed-Nego came from the midst of the fire."
~ Daniel 3:13-18, 25-26 (NKJV)

Also read: Entire chapter of Daniel 3

Story of Faith:
Can We Have Faith After Tragedy?
Ada Brownell

The baby was having trouble in the hospital delivery room. Every time my daughter pushed, the infant's oxygen shut off. The cord was too short and trapped between the child's head and the birth canal.

Our son–in-law stuck his head out the door. "Now would be a good time to pray."

60

His parents and we began to pray. My faith, I admit, was shaky as my mind imagined my daughter's grief if the baby were stillborn. Since we lost a child to an aggressive form of cancer, when I approach God's throne I'm aware He allows us to go through difficulty sometimes. Could I have faith after tragedy? I knew I believed God is the "rewarder of those who diligently seek Him" and "the worlds were framed by the word of God, so that the things that are seen were not made out of things which are visible." Both of those phrases come from Hebrews 11—the Bible's faith chapter.

So aware God was listening, I bound fear and loosed my faith. In moments, a cry came from the next room. The baby was fine.

Since then, I've increased Bible study. We've seen more miracles. Less than two years after that baby was born, during another pregnancy our daughter developed gall bladder trouble. The physician warned she might need surgery while pregnant. We prayed and she was able to wait until after the birth. Then our daughter was thought to have multiple sclerosis. Later tests showed she's fine. We've had many other miracles in our large family (one of them comfort after our oldest daughter's death), but I need to continue to build my faith.

Max Lucado paraphrases Hebrews 11 (NIV) in his article, "What Faith Sees": He says, "Faith is trusting what the eye can't see. Eyes see the prowling lion. Faith sees Daniel's angel. Eyes see storms. Faith sees Noah's rainbow. Your eyes see your faults. Your faith sees your Savior. Your eyes see your guilt. Your faith sees His blood." (http://www.thoughts-about-god.com)

I decided to research faith. This is what I found:

61

1. Our Creator wrapped faith in our DNA. Dr. Andrew Newberg, neuroscientist and author of "Why We Believe What We Believe," says our brains seem to have a special place for faith. He has tracked how the human brain processes religion and spirituality. It's all part of a new field called neurotheology. Newberg says the frontal lobe, the area right behind our foreheads, helps us focus our attention in prayer and meditation. The parietal lobe, located near the backs of our skulls, is the seat of our sensory information. He says this place in the brain is involved in that feeling of becoming part of something greater than oneself. The limbic system, nestled deep in the center, regulates our emotions and is responsible for feelings of awe and joy.

Newberg says similar areas of the brain are affected during prayer and meditation. He suggests brain scans may provide proof that our brains are built to believe in God. He says there may be universal features of the human mind that actually make it easier for us to believe in a higher power.

I believe people search for God because of the "God-shaped void" within. If they haven't heard the gospel or reject it, they worship the earth, an idol they know is nothing but a figure humans created, or devise their own religion—even making unbelief into doctrine.

2. God has given each person the ability to believe and his own lump of faith. *"For I say, through the grace given to me, to everyone who is among you, not to think of himself more highly than he ought to think, but to think soberly, as God has dealt to each one a measure of faith."* (Romans 12:3 NKJV).

3. Faith arises from the need to know our Heavenly Father. Since the Lord gave humankind a choice of whether to serve Him, God prevents us from "proving" He exists and leaves that and other vacancies for our faith to fill.

4. Faith comes through hearing the Word—the gospel. The Apostle Paul wrote *"Faith comes by hearing the message, and the message is heard through the word of Christ"* (Romans 10:17 NIV). *"All scripture is given by inspiration of God, and is profitable for doctrine, for reproof, for correction, for instruction in righteousness"* (2 Timothy 3:16 KJV).

5. Faith results from acting on what was heard. Romans 10:9 (NIV) says, *"If you declare with your mouth, 'Jesus is Lord,' and believe in your heart that God raised him from the dead, you will be saved."*

6. Faith comes through the will. We decide whether to believe God's Word, a false religion, or atheism. Everything about who we are, why we are here and where we are going takes faith. Yet it takes a leap—a decision.

7. Faith is created by combining belief with common-sense actions. James calls it "faith and works" (James 2:22).

8. Faith develops out of our hopes. We hope for something, but it takes faith to receive it.

9. Faith can come as a fruit and Gift of the Holy Spirit. (Galatians 5:22, 1 Corinthians 12:9).

10. Faith comes from a combination of our will to believe and the Holy Spirit's revelation. The Word must be planted, watered, and then our lives bear fruit.

Day #9:

Have you ever felt like you needed to do something a certain way in order to have faith? I know I have! Well, today I was reminded of the scripture in Hebrews 12:1-2 which talks about where our faith originates. Listen to this...

"Therefore we also, since we are surrounded by so great a cloud of witnesses, let us lay aside every weight, and the sin which so easily ensnares us, and let us run with endurance the race that is set before us, looking unto Jesus, the author and finisher of our faith, who for the joy that was set before Him endured the cross, despising the shame, and has sat down at the right hand of the throne of God." (NKJV)

Now, remember that Hebrews 11 is the "Hall of Faith" chapter which defines faith and describes many heroes of the faith from the Old Testament. So these verses come immediately after that chapter of faith.

And what does it say?

I love how these verses clearly tell us that Jesus is the "author and finisher of our faith." It is not up to us to muster up enough faith for the day. Our faith comes from Christ and not our own efforts.

If you are anything like me, you just breathed a big sigh of relief. Knowing that Jesus is the author and finisher of our faith takes the pressure off. It is not up to us.

So, I ask you today….are you trusting in Christ as the author and finisher of your faith or are you trusting in your own efforts to produce faith in your life?

"Don't trust to hold God's hand; let Him hold yours. Let Him do the holding, and you the trusting."
~ Hammer William Webb-Peploe

The Faith Challenge:

➤ Rest in the fact that Jesus is the author and finisher of your faith. If you are struggling with your faith, come to Him. Only through a personal relationship with Jesus will you truly live a life of faith.

Prayer of Faith:
Daniel

Lord, thank You for strengthening my faith in You. You are not a distant God, but instead, You desire a personal relationship with me. May our relationship continue to grow deeper with each passing day. Increase my love for You today.

Daniel had an unwavering faith in You. Even when his life was at risk, he still took the time to pray to You. His enemies came against him, but You spared his life when he was thrown into the lion's den. Why? Because he trusted in You.

Protect me from my enemies today in Jesus' name. May You be glorified in everything I do and say. And may my life demonstrate my deep trust in You. I love you so much. Amen.

"Then Daniel said to the king, 'O king, live forever! My God sent his angel and shut the lions' mouths, and they have not harmed me, because I was found blameless before him; and also before you, O king, I have done no harm.' Then the king was exceedingly glad, and commanded that Daniel be taken up out of the den. So Daniel was taken up out of the den, and no kind of harm was found on him, because he had trusted in his God."

~Daniel 6:21-23 (ESV)

Also read: Entire chapter of Daniel 6

Story of Faith:
Faith that Can Move Mountains
Amanda Penland

November and December of 2011 was exhausting. Trips to the ER and doctor were not uncommon. A week before Christmas my husband Tony was in the ER for the 3rd time due to severe dehydration from his new blood pressure medication. While the doctor asked him questions he told him about a lump he had recently discovered. A urologist was called in to run tests. The urologist was supposed to let him know the results as soon as possible. The next day he was sent home to rest.

He hadn't been his normal active self for a while due to the dehydration. I couldn't wait any longer. The suspense was killing me. So, on Christmas Eve I asked him, "Have you heard from the doctors yet?" I knew from the look he had on his face it wasn't good. He told me he got the letter a few days before. He just didn't want to tell me till after Christmas. He said he would need to have surgery to remove the mass. They weren't sure of the exact type or if it was spreading. I broke down.

On Christmas day, our pastor's wife gave out mustard seeds as the pastor spoke about having faith like a grain of mustard seed. I went right home and printed out the verse Matthew 17:20 (KJV): *"And Jesus said unto them, because of your unbelief: for verily I say unto you, If ye have faith as a grain of mustard seed, ye shall say unto this mountain, remove hence to yonder place; and it shall remove; and nothing shall be impossible unto you."*

I posted it with the mustard seed on our fridge. Every time we passed by it we would pray and even touch the seed. I got on my knees telling God I had faith that he would heal Tony. I knew He could confine his cancer and keep it from spreading to the rest of his body. I asked God to be with the doctors and help them to remove all the cancer from his body.

We went to talk with the urologist about the upcoming procedure and the type of testicular cancer it could be. I was so numb and I hurt so much I couldn't comprehend. When you hurt it's hard not to doubt. When we got home the tears fell. Tony and I held each other and prayed. A week before his surgery, praise God, his tumor moved! On January 10, 2012 the doctors removed it all. The urologist said it was confined only to that one area. Tony has so far been cancer free since his surgery.

Day #10:

My initial goal was to go through the 21 days of faith challenge for 21 days in a row. However, I had an unexpected detour in this journey. A little over a month ago, I realized that I had an overuse injury from spending too much time working on the computer. My forearms were sore, my neck and shoulders were sore and I knew I needed to take a break from the computer. So for the past month, I have put this challenge on hold.

I have to admit that when I first realized my body was breaking down from overuse on the computer, my initial reaction was to worry. After all, my job now requires that I spend 90% of my day on the computer. So if I cannot use a computer, then I cannot work. If I cannot work, we may not be able to pay our bills. You can see where this quickly leads.

However, God immediately brought to my mind this faith challenge and I knew I wanted to handle this "crisis" differently and trust God to provide for us. So I brought the situation to God in prayer. As I did, I faced the fact that my body was not a machine and that I was going to need to make some changes in order for my body to heal and for me to continue my work.

And an interesting thing happened.

As I faced the facts and surrendered them to God, emotions began to surface. I was no longer able to deny what was happening. I allowed myself to cry and grieve as I trusted God with my physical health and my finances. It was a healthy release of emotions. Instead of responding with worry and denial, I was able to feel my emotions and surrender the situation to God in faith.

And it made me think of one of the "heroes of the faith" that we read about in Hebrews 11. His name is Abraham.

Romans 4:19-22 says, *"Without weakening in his faith, he (Abraham) faced the fact that his body was as good as dead—since he was about a hundred years old—and that Sarah's womb was also dead. Yet he did not waver through unbelief regarding the promise of God, but was strengthened in his faith and gave glory to God, being fully persuaded that God had power to do what he had promised. This is why 'it was credited to him as righteousness.'"* (NIV)

So even as Abraham faced the fact that his body was as good as dead, he did not waver through unbelief regarding the promise of God that he would have a child but instead was strengthened in his faith. Amazing, isn't it? And that is how I want to respond as well. I want to be able to face the facts and yet not be weakened in my faith.

I want to respond by trusting God.

"Christians (as well as everyone else) have a tendency to try building a life in which faith is unnecessary. We establish a comfort zone where everything is in our control, but this is not pleasing to God. God will allow things into our lives that drive us to utter dependence upon him. Then we see His power and His glory."

~Henry Blackaby

The Faith Challenge:

➢ When a crisis comes into your life, what is your initial reaction? Is it worry, panic or denial? Or are you able to face the facts and trust God in faith with your circumstances?

➢ Write out the Scripture from Romans 4:19-22 and post it somewhere that you will see it every day. Read it every day and ask God to help you respond in a similar way the next time you face a crisis.

Prayer of Faith:
Woman Healed

I feel desperate for you today, Lord. I am hard pressed on every side, but not crushed; perplexed but not in despair; struck down, but not destroyed. And yet I know You are with me through every dark trial that I walk through.

Like the woman who had been bleeding for 12 years and was desperate to be healed, I am desperate for You. She knew that You had the power to heal her and she believed that if she simply touched the hem of Your garment, she would be healed. And she was healed. Instantly. You said her faith made her well.

And so today I reach out for you. I know that no one else has the answers or the ability to heal me but You. You are the Alpha and Omega; the Beginning and the End. I thank you for giving me the faith to simply reach for You. May You bring healing to me today where I need it. I pray all this in Jesus' name, Amen.

*"We are hard pressed on every side, but not crushed;
perplexed, but not in despair; persecuted, but not abandoned;
struck down, but not destroyed."*
~ 2 Corinthians 4:8-9 (NIV)

*"As Jesus went, the people pressed around him. And there was
a woman who had had a discharge of blood for twelve years,
and though she had spent all her living on physicians, she
could not be healed by anyone. She came up behind him and
touched the fringe of his garment, and immediately her
discharge of blood ceased. And Jesus said, 'Who was it that
touched me?' When all denied it, Peter said, 'Master, the
crowds surround you and are pressing in on you!' But Jesus
said, 'Someone touched me, for I perceive that power has
gone out from me.' And when the woman saw that she was not
hidden, she came trembling, and falling down before him
declared in the presence of all the people why she had touched
him, and how she had been immediately healed. And he said to
her, 'Daughter, your faith has made you well; go in peace.'"*
~ Luke 4:42-48 (ESV)

*"I am the Alpha and the Omega, the First and the Last, the
Beginning and the End."*
~ Revelation 22:13 (NLT)

Story of Faith:
Three Ways to Exchange Fear for Faith
Janet Perez Eckles

The other day while my fingers danced on my keyboard,
suddenly something happened. My muscles tightened. "Cindi,
I don't know what's wrong," I wrote to my friend and ministry
partner. "I'm stuck, really stuck. My computer says there's no
room on the disk and I'm out of memory."

71

Even from far away, she resolved the crisis. "Sometimes," she wrote gently, "this can happen when you have too many windows open."

Duh! That's exactly what happened. I, the queen of multi-tasking, had so many windows open at once that a mighty draft was probably blowing my way.

Why do we do that? It's insane. We open windows in life too—our kids do something off-the-wall for the umpteenth time, we open the window of worry. When will they ever learn! Money problems don't let up, so we open the window of anxiety. The doctor's office leaves a message, "We found something abnormal in the test." We open the window of fear. Our spouse still won't understand us; we fling open the window of anger.

Then our life gets stuck, no more memory of joy. The files where peace was stored can't be accessed. And the folder of security is empty.

Frustration led me to find a 3-step solution:

1.) Take a deep breath, look up. The God of the universe is watching. He's listening and ready to point to the solution.

2.) Pull emotionally away from all those open windows.

3.) Inhale His comfort, repeat His promise and know that, *"Though I am surrounded by troubles, you will bring me safely through them"* (Psalm 138:7, The LB-Paraphrased).

Father, in the midst of fear that fuels my stress, how comforting it is to know that You, with Your mighty power, will bring me safely through all those stages. Teach me to trust in You, in your timing and in Your ways, as You show me how to purposefully close the window of fear brought on by adversity. In Jesus's name, Amen.

Day #11:

I was thinking the other day about things in my life that I put my faith in without questioning. For example, when I go to sit in a chair, I have faith in gravity. I also have faith that the chair will hold me as I put my full weight into it. When I eat my food each day, I have faith that it is not poisoned. I have faith each month that I will receive a royalty paycheck for my books that have sold.

So, if I can have faith in simple things like this, why is it difficult for me to have faith in God's promises? God shares His promises with us in His Word, the Bible. But do we really believe them?

2 Corinthians 1:20 tells us, *"For all the promises of God in Him are Yes, and in Him Amen, to the glory of God through us."* (NKJV)

What are some of the promises of God in the Bible? Here are just a few...

- Salvation comes through Jesus. (John 3:16, John 14:6)

- When we abide in Christ, we will bear much fruit. (John 15:5)

- We are heirs of God and co-heirs with Christ. (Romans 8:16-17)

- In this world we will have trouble, but Christ has overcome the world. (John 16:33)

- Jesus is the author and finisher of our faith. (Hebrews 12:1-2)

- Nothing can separate us from the love of Christ. (Romans 8:38-39)

- One day, in heaven, there will be no more death, sorrow, crying or pain. (Revelation 21:4)

- God who began a good work in us is faithful to complete it. (Philippians 1:6)

- God will provide for our needs when we put Him first in our lives. (Matthew 6:33)

I have learned that I can trust and have faith in the promises of God in the Bible. However, the first step for me was being able to trust the Bible.

"The Bible is a checkbook. When you said yes to Jesus Christ, many promises were deposited to your credit at that very moment, and they were signed by the Lord Jesus Himself. But now you have to cash your checks in order to profit by them. When you come upon such a promise and say, 'Thank you, Lord, I accept this,' then you have cashed a check, and that very day you'll be richer than you were the day before."
~ Corrie ten Boom

The Faith Challenge:

➢ What you believe about God's Word, the Bible, will make a huge difference in how you live your life. So, today, reflect on this question…do you have faith in the promises of God through the Bible? Do you believe the Bible is absolute truth and has power for your life today? Or is the Bible simply a history book to you?

➢ Take a few minutes today to read the article I wrote several years ago about why I trust the Bible. I also share a song by Sanctus Real that has encouraged me titled "Promises." Read the article and listen to the song here: www.bodyandsoulpublishing.com/promises

Prayer of Faith:
Blind Men

Lord, sometimes I simply need to ask You for what I need instead of worrying or complaining. Increase my faith in Your ability to meet my needs just like the blind men sitting along the roadside that came to You with their need and told You specifically what they wanted. They wanted their sight and You chose to heal them that day.

Your word says we do not have because we have not asked You. Therefore, today I come to You asking You for what I need - _____ (insert your request here).

Help me to put my trust in You and not my own self-sufficiency. Empower me to depend on You and come to You first asking for what I need before I go to others or try to figure it out myself. I love You Lord, Amen.

"As Jesus and his disciples were leaving Jericho, a large crowd followed him. Two blind men were sitting by the roadside, and when they heard that Jesus was going by, they shouted, 'Lord, Son of David, have mercy on us!' The crowd

rebuked them and told them to be quiet, but they shouted all
the louder, 'Lord, Son of David, have mercy on us!' Jesus
stopped and called them. 'What do you want me to do for
you?' he asked. 'Lord,' they answered, 'we want our sight.'
Jesus had compassion on them and touched their eyes.
Immediately they received their sight and followed him."
~ Matthew 20:29-34 (NIV)

"You do not have because you do not ask God."
~ James 4:2b (NIV)

Story of Faith:
Like Pine, Like Pain
Jorja Davis

Last week a crash of thunder in the night marked the moment when all our plans for the next day would make an abrupt shift. It was the moment when an eighty-foot pine tree went twisting and crashing and fell across our backyard. Rather than turning the soil in the garden for planting pumpkins with the grandchildren, my husband cleaned and oiled the chain-saw to remove the tree lying across the children's garden. That sudden shift of priority reminded me of a not-so-subtle shift, when after three months of aggressive treatment for pain, the word cure disappeared and the word management took its place. It was a shock, a thunderclap.

Eighteen years ago, I had minor surgery. Four weeks after the surgery, my life came crashing down around me. I developed a major complication that would soon become chronic and then intractable. Reflex Sympathetic Dystrophy created profound changes that overshadowed my life and living. Instead of sewing 5000 seed pearls on our older daughter's wedding dress and packing for our last military tour in

77

Germany, almost every day I rode 80 miles round trip in excruciating, burning pain to the John Hopkins Medical Research Hospital's Pain Management Clinic.

Somehow among all the lumbar sympathetic blocks that had their own pain, I found myself leaning more and more into Jesus' arms. Every time, I had to sign a sheet of paper explaining the possible outcomes of the treatment. The last phrase was always "even death." I knew I won either way, but thank goodness I learned to put my head on Jesus' shoulder and let Him wrap His arms around me, especially on the day when all the students came to observe. In addition to the x-rays he used to help position the needle, the doctor used contrast dye so the students could better see the procedure. It turned out I was allergic to the dye. No better place to disappear into anaphylaxis than in a room with 8 doctors, being held by the Great Physician.

When we arrived in Germany, the blocks were administered by an anesthesiologist in the surgical recovery room in the Army Hospital, where all injured soldiers are triaged and treated before returning to their units or home countries. He did not use x-ray. Because he had worked twenty years in military hospitals, he had done thousands of lumbar sympathetic blocks on soldiers who had lost limbs, suffered crush traumas, or gunshot wounds. I found myself burying my head in Jesus' shoulder, grasping two-fists-full of his garments. Praying aloud through every treatment right up to the day the nurses were putting up Christmas decorations.

This was the day the interns rotated into the recovery room. The anesthesiologist laughed and joked as he began the procedure. This time the doctor nicked a blood vessel. The steroids and lidocaine rushed to my heart, my lungs, and my brain. The room began to spin, I could see fireworks on the ceiling, and I could not breathe. The anesthesiologist called for saline fluid and a nurse to start an IV in my arm. Quietly at first and then increasing in volume I heard Amy Grant singing Breath of Heaven. "Breath of heaven hold me together, be forever near me. Hold me together. Hold me." God's presence has never been more real or palpable.

Like taking a chainsaw to the tree, eighteen years of living with chronic pain has cut my self-identity down to holy size…to what God sees. My day planner has been converted from allotments of time to chunks of energy. My priorities have tumbled from many to one at a time. Before pain consumed my days and nights, I often forgot I am not defined by what I do, but by who and whose I am. Pain is, among other things, clarifying.

Everything that is planned or scheduled will take time and energy. And even if I know how much energy is needed, I will not know how much energy I will have to spend until I wake up. I know it will take two hours to stretch my muscles and get my stiff joints moving. If I use those two hours to stretch my body and direct my focus away from pain toward God, I stay more relaxed and more ready to deal with scheduled events and falling trees.

The pain remains. The deterioration of body continues. Some mornings my Bible is too heavy to hold. Some mornings my fingers will not turn a page. Some mornings I just light a candle scented with myrrh and sit and immerse myself in the smell of a gift of pain and memory--and in words of hope remembered:

"Be still and know that I am God." (Psalm 46:10 NIV)

"Come to me all you who are weary." (Matthew 11:28 NIV)

The principles haven't changed. They are just narrowed from plural to singular:

- balance goal and priority;
- set a manageable task according to available energy;
- leave some slack to deal with the unexpected – such as fallen trees.

The tree fell a week ago. A large part of it still lies across the backyard right up to the edge of the pumpkin patch. I can smell the pine when the back door is opened. The dark earth-bound roots are turning a rain-washed gray. Someday my husband will return to the task of sawing the rest into movable chunks. The tree will be cut and gone only when it becomes the priority, goal, and critical task of the day. Today we need to plant pumpkin seeds with the grandchildren.

Like pine, like pain, well-managed, I pray.

Day #12:

As I have already shared with you, this last year was a difficult year for me. I finally realized that I needed to reach out for help. Our church offers free Biblical counseling and so I decided to set up an appointment. I ended up attending only two sessions, but God used them powerfully in my life.

During one of my sessions, I had an "ah ha" moment as we looked at the story of the feeding of the 5,000 in John 6:4-14 which you can read below.

"The Jewish Passover Festival was near. When Jesus looked up and saw a great crowd coming toward him, He said to Philip, 'Where shall we buy bread for these people to eat?' He asked this only to test him, for He already had in mind what He was going to do.

Philip answered Him, 'It would take more than half a year's wages to buy enough bread for each one to have a bite!'

Another of His disciples, Andrew, Simon Peter's brother, spoke up, 'Here is a boy with five small barley loaves and two small fish, but how far will they go among so many?'

Jesus said, 'Have the people sit down.' There was plenty of grass in that place, and they sat down (about five thousand men were there). Jesus then took the loaves, gave thanks, and distributed to those who were seated as much as they wanted. He did the same with the fish. When they had all had enough to eat, He said to His disciples, 'Gather the pieces that are left over. Let nothing be wasted.' So they gathered them and filled twelve baskets with the pieces of the five barley loaves left over by those who had eaten. After the people saw the sign Jesus performed, they began to say, 'Surely this is the Prophet who is to come into the world.'" (NIV)

We see that Phillip and Andrew had two very different responses to Jesus' question on how to feed the thousands of people that had gathered to hear His teachings.

    1.) Phillip looked at the facts and made statements based only on what he could see. "It would take more than half a year's wages to buy enough bread for each one to have a bite!"

    2.) Andrew surrendered the little resources he had to Jesus who then multiplied them to provide above and beyond what was needed.

Who do you relate to more in this story? For me, I relate more to Philip. I am naturally a problem solver and see the facts. I tend to look at a situation realistically and then try to figure out what it will take to get from A to B. However, this limits what God can do in the situation.

Instead, I want to be more like Andrew and in faith surrender the little resources I do have to Jesus and allow Him to multiply them. This does not mean that Jesus is a "genie in a bottle" to do my bidding. It simply means that I surrender my circumstances and what I do have to Jesus and then allow Him to take the lead. This also means that I am not limited by what I see but realize that Jesus is able to do more than I can ask or imagine. (Ephesians 3:20)

"God is not some little genie or a vending machine. And (He) is not just worth it because He makes your life all better, but

He's with you. God wants so much more for your life than fine."

~ Jim Britts

The Faith Challenge:

> In the story that we read above, do you relate more to Philip or Andrew and why?

> When faced with an impossible situation, I encourage you to approach it like Andrew did…bringing what you do have to Jesus and asking Him to do the rest. Then listen to God and obey Him. In the story above, the disciples were active participants in distributing the food. And in a similar way, God may ask you to take action in a specific way in your circumstances.

The Bible tells us that faith without works is dead (James 2:17). However, we want our actions to be led by God and not simply our own ideas. This means that we need to spend time in prayer bringing our requests to God, but also spend time in prayer listening to Him as well. This is very difficult in our fast-paced, media driven culture. However, spending time in silence listening to God is so necessary for a growing relationship with Him and a life of faith.

Prayer of Faith:
Boy's Father

Lord, I thank You for another day. Although this life is full of challenges and difficulties I know that the one constant in my life is You. You have promised to never leave me or forsake me.

Sometimes when I'm faced with a trial, my faith wavers. Similar to the boy's father who said *"IF you can do anything have compassion on us and help us,"* I sometimes doubt You. I need to be reminded of the response You gave that boy's father that day…

"If you can! All things are possible for one who believes."

Even though You may not choose to answer my prayers in the ways I would like them to be answered, You always have the power to do above and beyond anything that I can think or imagine.

And so today, I pray the same prayer that father prayed…Lord, I do believe; help my unbelief! Thank You for continuing to do Your work in my heart and my life. Amen.

"Never will I leave you; never will I forsake you."
~ Hebrews 13:5 (NIV)

"And Jesus asked his father, 'How long has this been happening to him?" And he said, "From childhood. And it has often cast him into fire and into water, to destroy him. But if you can do anything, have compassion on us and help us.' And Jesus said to him, 'If you can! All things are possible for one who believes.' Immediately the father of the child cried out and said, 'I believe; help my unbelief!' And when Jesus saw that a crowd came running together, he rebuked the unclean spirit, saying to it, 'You mute and deaf spirit, I command you, come out of him and never enter him again.' And after crying out and convulsing him terribly, it came out, and the boy was

like a corpse, so that most of them said, 'He is dead.' But
Jesus took him by the hand and lifted him up, and he arose."
~ Mark 9:21-27 (ESV)

"Now to him who is able to do immeasurably more than all we
ask or imagine, according to his power that is at work within
us, to him be glory in the church and in Christ Jesus
throughout all generations, for ever and ever! Amen."
~ Ephesians 3:20-21 (NIV)

Story of Faith:
No Limits

Kim Bookmyer

"For nothing is impossible with God."
~ Luke 1:37 (NLT)

The Lord has been patiently trying to teach me the TRUTH of
this verse over the last several years. Recently He took me on
a mission trip to Nicaragua to show me once again that with
Him there are NO LIMITS!

With God - there are NO language barriers, age barriers,
cultural barriers, physical barriers, economic barriers,
relationship barriers, denominational barriers, _____(fill in
the blank). When we put our trust in Him, He is well able to
take down all of those barriers so that we may experience His
unconditional, passionate love for all people!

I may have a language barrier as I don't speak Spanish BUT
God doesn't! He was showing me that His love can be
communicated in a smile, a touch, through a provision of food,
an embrace, a prayer, worship. God brought to us Nicaraguans
who love Jesus and traveled with us to be our interpreters.
Often though there were not enough interpreters and we were

dependent on the Holy Spirit to lead us and guide us as we prayed for people.

God understands all languages. As we prayed for people it was amazing to watch God break through walls that were in their lives and to bring healing and comfort to them. We were complete strangers; asking God to touch them at the root of their pain, doubt, fear, brokenness. And right in front of us, we could see the power of the Holy Spirit consuming them. A person's countenance would completely change and after prayer there would be an unspeakable joy; a transformed life! A new follower of Christ or a hurting brother or sister who left knowing that God was their provider, comforter, healer! We may not have known what happened but the Creator who "knit them together fearfully and wonderfully" (Psalm 139:13-14 paraphrased) sure touched them. There are NO LIMITS with God.

In the United States we've put up a barrier for God in our educational system. In Nicaragua, it is still permissible to come into the public schools and share the gospel message and pray with the students. So often we did our outreach in public schools. The students shared music, dramas and testimonies of how the Lord has changed their lives and then there would be an altar call for prayer. They were hungry for God and many would come for prayer!

At one of the schools, I noticed a couple teachers standing in a doorway. I felt led to go pray with them. After finding someone to ask them if they would like prayer, one teacher left. I was wondering what happened but in a moment I found out that she was getting the principal and soon the entire teaching staff was standing in the office wanting prayer. God had made a way for me, a former 5th grade teacher from Ohio, to pray for these beautiful teachers in Nicaragua! Only God knew that one day I would be in Nicaragua praying with other teachers! There are NO LIMITS with God in the school systems.

We may have put up barriers in our government and in the church but God was showing me His heart to be involved! Several years ago, God showed me that as believers we are called to uplift our pastors in prayer and to encourage them in the Lord for they have a difficult job shepherding us sheep and to also pray for our governmental leaders for His wisdom. We were in one community where the mayor, a man of God, had coordinated with the local pastors to seek God together. We were at the mayors' office for lunch and 12 pastors (from different denominations) had taken the day to spend with us. They traveled to the different schools and then we were all part of an evangelistic crusade for the entire community that evening where there must have been 900 people worshiping God together. God provided me an opportunity to pray with the pastors. One shared with me how the Lord has been bringing unity to their community by bringing the pastors together. They meet to pray with one another regularly including the mayor! Where there is unity, God will command the blessing! There are NO LIMITS with God in the government or the church.

One day, we were waiting to cross a river to get to one of the villages where we were sharing the good news of Jesus Christ and feeding the children. I was pondering how I was going to cross the river. The youth were jumping to the other side but I was sizing up the width and thinking...I'm getting wet! Then in the distance I could see this man, carrying a plank. He made a bridge for the remainder of us to cross. God provides a way. Seeing that man made me think of Jesus who provides the way...the way to a relationship with our Creator! He carried a cross, was crucified and lives again so that we may cross over....effortlessly because of His great sacrifice. He is the God that transcends all barriers and it is only because of His

Son, Jesus Christ's death, resurrection and ascension that all things are possible with Him. It is because He did not leave us alone but gave us Himself in the person of the Holy Spirit to live within us now...so that we may have LIFE ABUNDANTLY now and forevermore!

Brothers and sisters in Christ, with God there are NO LIMITS! Seek Him with all that you are. Ask Him every morning to break your heart over the things that break His heart and to fill your heart with His love, to give you eyes to see as He sees and ears to hear His voice above all the other voices in the world. He has great plans for you....be amazed at where and how the Father desires to use you for His glory...for His Kingdom purposes. This mom from Ohio is amazed to see how the Lord has transformed me and took me to Nicaragua to share His love with others. For there is NOTHING that is impossible with God! (Luke 1:37) He is LIMITLESS! Believe that there are NO LIMITS with God!

Day #13:

I want to share a picture that I believe God gave to me as I was meditating on the definition of faith recently.

Placing my faith in God is like handing my car keys to Him. I no longer have control, but look to Him for guidance. And because God now holds the keys to my car, He decides when we leave, He decides when to start the car, He decides where we go, etc.

And I have to admit, that as I think about this illustration, I feel uncomfortable. Why? Well, first of all, it is difficult for me to give up complete control. Secondly, it feels like I am doing nothing. I like to be an active participant and be able to do something.

But, it all comes back to trust. Do I trust God?

I need to know and believe that God does not want to destroy my life. On the contrary, He has a plan for me, to prosper me and not to harm me (Jeremiah 29:11). He wants to take me on the ride of my life...if only I will give Him the car keys.

The Bible says in John 14:12, *"Very truly I tell you, whoever believes in Me will do the works I have been doing, and they will do even greater things than these, because I am going to the Father."* (NIV)

When we decide to give the "car keys" of our life over to God and believe in Him in faith, He will do amazing things through our lives. Let's choose to live a life of faith and not miss anything He has for us!

"The world has yet to see what God can do with a man (or woman) *fully consecrated to Him. By God's help, I aim to be that man."*

~ Dwight L. Moody (my insertion)

The Faith Challenge:

➢ Have you surrendered the "keys" of your life to God? Or are you still holding on and the one in control? Ultimately, Jesus does not want to simply be part of our lives, like one slice of pumpkin pie, He wants to be the main ingredient of our lives. He wants to be the pumpkin in our pumpkin pie. He wants to be Lord of our lives.

➢ Ask God if there is any area of your life that you need to fully surrender to Him. If you already have a personal relationship with Jesus Christ, then this could be a relationship, finances, your job, material possessions, your time, etc. Pray a prayer of surrender and visualize yourself handing the keys of your life in that area over to God.

However, if you have never surrendered your life fully to Jesus to make Him Lord of your life, I encourage you to do so today. There are many people that know about Jesus, can quote Bible verses and/or attend church regularly, but do not know Jesus on a personal level as their Lord and Savior. If that is the case for you, today can be the day of your salvation. There are no magic words to pray; you simply ask Jesus to forgive you of your sins, acknowledge that He is the only way to God, and then start living your life for Him.

If you do not know where to start you can pray this simple prayer: "Dear Lord Jesus, I know that I am a sinner and need Your forgiveness. I believe that You died for my sins. I want to turn from my sins. I now invite You to come into my heart and life. I want to trust and follow You as Lord and Savior. In Jesus' name. Amen."

If you are making this step for the first time, contact me and let me know. You can e-mail us here: Bodyandsoulpublishing.com/contact.

We want to pray for you and send you some resources to help you grow in your relationship with Jesus.

If you want to know more or still have questions about a relationship with Jesus, I encourage you to read this article I wrote on my website here: www.bodyandsoulpublishing.com/jesus.

Prayer of Faith: Centurion

Jesus, as I read about Your life in the Bible, I grow to know You better. One of the things You looked for and commended in people was their faith. In fact, Your word tells us that without faith it is impossible to please You.

There was a centurion who came to You and asked You to heal his servant. He knew that You had the authority to heal his servant even at a distance. Just like the centurion would command those under his authority to do something and they would do it, he believed You could simply say the word and in the authority given to You by God, his servant would be healed. And his servant was healed that very hour.

Lord, help to expand my faith in You today. Give me faith like this centurion to believe that Your authority has no boundaries. Remove any doubt in my mind and my heart today in Jesus' name. Amen.

"And without faith it is impossible to please Him, for whoever would draw near to God must believe that He exists and that He rewards those who seek Him."
~ Hebrews 11:6 (ESV)

"Now when Jesus had entered Capernaum, a centurion came to Him, pleading with Him, saying, 'Lord, my servant is lying at home paralyzed, dreadfully tormented.' And Jesus said to him, 'I will come and heal him.' The centurion answered and said, 'Lord, I am not worthy that You should come under my roof. But only speak a word, and my servant will be healed. For I also am a man under authority, having soldiers under me. And I say to this one, 'Go,' and he goes; and to another, 'Come,' and he comes; and to my servant, 'Do this,' and he does it.' When Jesus heard it, He marveled, and said to those who followed, 'Assuredly, I say to you, I have not found such great faith, not even in Israel! And I say to you that many will come from east and west, and sit down with Abraham, Isaac, and Jacob in the kingdom of heaven. But the sons of the kingdom will be cast out into outer darkness. There will be weeping and gnashing of teeth.' Then Jesus said to the centurion, 'Go your way; and as you have believed, so let it be done for you.' And his servant was healed that same hour."
~Matthew 8:5-13 (NKJV)

Story of Faith:
Little Footsteps

Mark Moyers

Ah the good ole' days; I remember them fondly. It was a time when my relationship with God was just beginning to bloom. Everything was new, exciting, and full of possibilities. God was filling me with His word and His Spirit as never before. Like a sweet summer day the glory of God washed over me, and everything was right with the world.

Thinking back on it, that was a pretty good weekend. Soon after, God enrolled me in spiritual boot camp. What's spiritual boot camp you say? Well, a good example is when God taught me the meaning of 2 Corinthians 5:7 (NIV)…

"For we live by faith, not by sight."

My lesson began with an ordinary evening out. A small group of people and I had gone out to eat one evening. A movie might have been involved as well, but to be honest, I really can't remember. You see, there was something else that captured my attention that night.

Over the course of the evening, somewhere between the breadsticks and the good-natured ribbing, the subject of abortion arose. It was a short exchange between a close friend and her boyfriend, only lasting for a moment. There were no heated exchanges or sharp disagreements, and yet, there was something about it that stood out to me. I was troubled by it, but I didn't understand why.

The evening passed quickly, but what I had experienced that night persisted long after the leftovers were gone. Try as I might, I couldn't shake the uneasiness I was feeling. Pushing it out of my thoughts was only temporary as it always had a way of creeping back in.

I tried to rationalize it, reason with whatever was happening. I knew my friend well; she was a Christian whose character matched her beliefs. She respected life and would never have an abortion. Yet, that wasn't enough to make it stop. On and on this went until it finally became clear what was happening.

In the night, in the middle of the darkness and the silence, that still small voice spoke deep into my spirit.

"Tell her."

Instantly I realize it had been God speaking to me all along, and now He wanted me to remind her of what she already knew. I didn't understand why, so I wrestled with God. I gave Him all the usual excuses – she's a Christian, she already knows, she might get angry with me – but He would have none of it. Just when I had almost completely pushed it out of my mind, He spoke again.

"Tell her!"

This time a little louder and more insistent. Again I offered my excuses and managed to push it down one more time – enough to make it comfortable for myself. Several times God spoke to me; each time was a bit louder and more insistent than the last. When He spoke my spirit would ring and my body would shudder making it impossible to miss His voice. This persisted until one final time.

"TELL HER!"

The prophet Jeremiah wrote that God's word was like a fire shut up in his bones (Jeremiah 20:9) and I wondered what it

94

was like to feel what Jeremiah was describing. When this last command came, I finally knew. And just like Jeremiah, I too could no longer hold what God had given me, so I relented.

I told God He would have to guide me in what to say, and He did just that. But out of fear I couldn't speak to her directly. If you have ever tried to deliver God's message to someone, you would know why. So I wrote it in a letter and mailed it.

A couple weeks later I received a phone call; she had called to talk about what I wrote. She wasn't angry, but she was a bit confused, much like me. I assured her I already knew what she believed, but I felt the need to remind her. She accepted that, and after some small talk we parted once again.

As you might have guessed, our conversation didn't bring me any clarity. I still had no idea what the purpose of this was, or even if there was a purpose. And after we hung up I thought to myself, "I wonder why God had me do that." Immediately, God spoke once again.

"She is going to have a baby."

What?! God, how? She isn't married, she isn't even engaged! Plus she is saving herself for marriage! I had just received an answer from God about "why" – a rather rare answer to receive – and it only brought me more questions. So, I did what any other rational person would do in my position – I decided I must be crazy and did my best to forget about it. And it worked. That is, until the tables were turned.

Months later, it was my turn to receive something in the mail. It was... a wedding invitation. Yes, you guessed it – my friend and her boyfriend, the same one that was with us that night, were getting married. Once I regained consciousness the natural line of questioning ensued. Could it really be? Was God's Word fulfilled? Is she... is she really?

For months I wondered, right up until the day of the wedding. As the time drew near I counted the moments.

Tick... I arrive at the church.
Tock... I'm standing in the foyer.
Tick... I make my way to a pew – an aisle seat.
Tock... The groom and groomsmen enter.
Tick... The music starts.
Tock... The sanctuary doors open...

She's thin! Hallelujah! Finally, closure! What a relief, I must have been wrong, and I'm glad. Now I can put this whole thing behind me, and I will never have to deal with anything like this ever again.

Six weeks after the wedding I had the chance to talk with my newly married friend on the phone. We spoke about how the wedding went, where they went on their honeymoon, and "oh by the way, did I mention I'm pregnant?" What!? Already? "Yep, that quickly." She continued, "...and my husband wants me to have an abortion."

Instantly, all of the pieces fall into place. Humbled, and in awe of God's amazing goodness, we hang up and I hear that still small voice one more time.

"See?"

Looking back, it was such a small step of faith that pales in comparison to some of the things God has had me do since. But of course, first steps always do. On that day, no mountains were moved, no seas were parted, but one blind man received his sight. The oh-so-small amount of discomfort I experienced paled in comparison to the priceless lesson I learned.

I don't know if what God directed me to do changed the course of events, but I don't have to know, for we walk by faith, not by sight. What I do know is, God knows what He is doing, and my friend's baby girl is doing just fine.

Day #14:

It can be easy to say that we trust in God, but how do we truly know that we are relying on Him?

My husband and I were short-term missionaries in the country of Belize, Central America for two years. When we arrived in Belize, we had a general idea of the ministry we would be involved in; however, we did not know the details of how everything would work out.

I remember the first few months as we were getting adjusted, we continued to pray for doors to open for us. We waited, and waited, and waited. At least that is what it felt like to me. During this waiting time, my husband, CJ, wrote out the following quote in big block letters and posted it on our kitchen wall where we would see it every day.

Here is the quote:

"Prayer is the proof we are relying on God."

And it is so true.

Prayer is the proof we are relying on God and not on ourselves. Eventually, my husband decided to undergo three days of prayer and fasting. During those few days of seeking God through prayer and fasting, God gave CJ a message that he then shared with over 10,000 Belizean students that year. Not only did God open the doors for ministry in schools in every district in Belize, He also gave CJ the opportunity to share a message about sexual purity that contained the gospel and impacted many lives. Prayer is powerful.

"Prayer is not asking. Prayer is putting oneself in the hands of God, at His disposition, and listening to His voice in the depth of our hearts."

~ Mother Teresa

"Any concern too small to be turned into a prayer is too small to be made into a burden."

~ Corrie ten Boom

The Faith Challenge:

➢ How is your prayer life? It is so easy to allow busyness to take over our lives, isn't it? I encourage you to spend intentional time connecting with God through prayer today. This could include a longer more intimate prayer time in the morning, short prayers all throughout the day, journaling out your prayers, etc. Then, continue coming to God day after day in prayer until it is a habit. Not a legalistic habit, but a habit that leads to a greater dependence and reliance on God...a habit that leads to a life of faith.

Prayer of Faith:
Mary

Father, there are so many examples of people who lived a life of faith in the Bible. I am encouraged to know they are ordinary people just like me. I do not need to be a "super Christian" in order to have faith. I simply need You.

You chose Mary to be the mother of Your son, Jesus. When Your Angel gave her the news, Mary did have a couple questions. However, her questions were not asked from a spirit of doubt. In the end, Mary said to your messenger, "*may it be to me as you have said,*" indicating her surrendered heart and faith in Your plan.

Help me to surrender my life to You today. Give me the faith to trust Your plans for me. As Jesus said in the garden of Gethsemane, "*not my will, but Yours, be done,*" May that also be my prayer today. I love you, Lord. Amen.

"In the sixth month the angel Gabriel was sent from God to a city of Galilee named Nazareth, to a virgin betrothed to a man whose name was Joseph, of the house of David. And the virgin's name was Mary. And he came to her and said, 'Greetings, O favored one, the Lord is with you!' But she was greatly troubled at the saying, and tried to discern what sort of greeting this might be. And the angel said to her, 'Do not be afraid, Mary, for you have found favor with God. And behold, you will conceive in your womb and bear a son, and you shall call his name Jesus. He will be great and will be called the Son of the Most High. And the Lord God will give to him the throne of his father David, and he will reign over the house of Jacob forever, and of his kingdom there will be no end.'

And Mary said to the angel, 'How will this be, since I am a virgin?'

And the angel answered her, 'The Holy Spirit will come upon you, and the power of the Most High will overshadow you; therefore the child to be born will be called holy—the Son of God. And behold, your relative Elizabeth in her old age has also conceived a son, and this is the sixth month with her who was called barren. For nothing will be impossible with God.'

And Mary said, 'Behold, I am the servant of the Lord; let it be to me according to your word." And the angel departed from her.'"

~ Luke 1:26-38 (ESV)

"Father, if you are willing, remove this cup from me. Nevertheless, not my will, but yours, be done."

~Luke 22:42 (ESV)

Story of Faith:
Desires of the Heart

Lilly Maytree

My husband and I fell in love with boats early in our marriage, and owned several over the years. They ranged from our first twenty-three-foot sailboat on a nearby lake, to an ocean-going sloop twice that size when our children were teenagers and made up a great crew. Having tried pretty much everything, we dreamed of having a traditional ketch with classic lines, small enough for just the two of us to handle, but could still go anywhere in the world.

Of course, that kind was incredibly expensive, and life distracted us with many things that were more important. However, when the freedom of retirement came along, we started dreaming, again. Then, one summer, we set out to discover if "divine appointments" were real (I had recently written a novel on that theme), and unknowingly embarked on the adventure of a lifetime.

It began as a book tour. But it was more than that, really, because we didn't exactly know where we were going, or what our final destination would be. And because it was as much a mystery to us as anyone else, we called it a "mystery tour."

Did God have any real divine appointments lined up for us? And if so, how would we recognize them?

I've heard when traveling through new territory, it's best to follow someone who knows where they're going. So, we began looking for the "footsteps of God" ahead of us, in order to make sure we stayed to the right path. These were the little things that worked out with such perfect timing that we couldn't possibly have arranged ourselves. We had been rescued this way during many emergencies of our lives and called them miracles because there was simply no other way to explain them. Could the same thing work for dreams?

Next thing we knew, that long ago dream became very intense. But, living on a fixed income, we were in no position to buy a sailboat. Still, times being what they were, there might be someone out there who desperately needed to get rid of one. And one of the surest signs of "God's footsteps" was that His provisions usually met the needs of more than just us at the same time. So, we began to look from one end of the state to the other, at any and all boats that might fit the requirements.

First of all, there would have to be no money down, because we didn't have any. In fact, we had to rent our house out just to have enough in the budget for all the extra traveling it would take to find the thing. Then the owner would have to agree to carry financing on it, because we would never qualify for a bank loan. Not to mention we needed immediate possession since we had no place to live anymore. For heaven's sake, what were we thinking? And whose idea was it to blast it all over the internet by way of documentation so when this tremendous "miracle" happened, there would be no question it was God (and not us) who did it?

I could write an entire book on the potential this "mystery tour" had for being extremely embarrassing, but we won't go there. The important thing is that God did show up. The reason I know is because - well, for heaven's sake - I better not go there, either. Instead, I'll just jot down a "list of footsteps," and let you decide for yourself...

After weeks of looking, the only thing we found was where we would put a boat if we actually ever got one. It was a beautiful historical old waterfront on Liberty Bay.

We eventually ran out of gas money to look for more boats, so the Captain answered an ad in a Seattle newspaper for a part-time job to get some. It turned out to be next to Liberty Bay. It also turned out to have a couple hundred others who applied, but they chose my senior-age husband over all of them. What kind of job? Repair and replace roofing on commercial buildings. At an amazingly high wage.

During this "lull" in our hunt, I posted a picture of our original "dream boat" (on the blog) that I took from a sales catalog, simply because I had run out of real boats to look at. It was of a thirty-two foot Mariner ketch.

We stumbled onto a neglected version of that boat (right on Liberty Bay!) but it wasn't for sale. We tracked down the owner, anyway. Turns out he had health problems and couldn't keep it up. We made him an offer; he countered with A LOWER ONE, and AGREED TO ALL OUR TERMS.

There was a waiting list to get into the marina, but because the boat had been there for fourteen years, and the owner was friends with the harbor master, we got to stay in the same place for... half the current rate.

The Captain's job was less than a mile away from that location.

The former owner (also on a fixed income) was able to move into a better home with the extra money.

The boat cleaned up beautifully, and was completely paid off within a few months.

It was a thirty-two foot Mariner ketch... just like in the picture.

At this point you might wonder how all these amazingly "mysterious coincidences" affected our faith. Well, I'll tell you. The truth is, following in God's footsteps is extremely exciting. There's absolutely nothing else like it when it comes to adventure. So, we've decided we're not going home this year. Instead... we're going on.

"Delight yourself in the Lord: and he shall give you the desires of your heart. Commit your way to the Lord; trust also in him; and he shall bring it to pass."
~ Psalm 37:4-5 (NKJV)

Day #15:

Today I want to share with you the story of Mary and Martha.

"Now it happened as they went that He entered a certain village; and a certain woman named Martha welcomed Him into her house. And she had a sister called Mary, who also sat at Jesus' feet and heard His word. But Martha was distracted with much serving, and she approached Him and said, 'Lord, do You not care that my sister has left me to serve alone? Therefore tell her to help me.'

And Jesus answered and said to her, 'Martha, Martha, you are worried and troubled about many things. But one thing is needed, and Mary has chosen that good part, which will not be taken away from her.'"

~ Luke 10:38-42 (NKJV)

To be honest, I have always been able to relate to Martha. I am a hard worker and often have a long to-do list waiting for me each day. And some days, I neglect spending time with Jesus in order to start working on my to-do list. However, Jesus continues to remind me that the time I spend with Him sitting at His feet is so much more important than anything else.

It is similar to the story of a man chopping down a tree. He was working very hard, but not making much progress. Someone came up to him and realized that he was using a dull axe. They then recommended that he stop for a few minutes to sharpen his axe. However, the man pushed them aside saying he was too busy working to stop and sharpen his axe.

How foolish! If he would simply stop and sharpen his axe, he would have finished his work much sooner. And the same is true in our lives when it comes to prayer. When we spend time in prayer "sharpening our axe," our day will often go so much smoother and more efficiently as we allow God to guide our actions and our thoughts.

"If I had six hours to chop down a tree, I'd spend the first four hours sharpening the axe."

~ Abraham Lincoln.

"I have so much to do that I shall spend the first three hours in prayer."

~ Martin Luther

The Faith Challenge:

➢ Have you spent time "sharpening your axe" through prayer today? Would Jesus say to you: "Martha, Martha, (insert your name) you are worried and upset about many things, but only one thing is needed. Mary has chosen what is better, and it will not be taken from her."?

Take time to sit at Jesus' feet today even if you only have a few minutes.

➢ I like to play instrumental worship music sometimes to help draw me into the presence of God. David Delgado offers free instrumental worship music that you can download here: http://www.wordlessworship.com.

Prayer of Faith:
Paralytic

Lord, many days I am burdened by the needs of others. So many people are struggling with personal problems, health problems, financial issues, etc. However, I am not meant to carry their burdens alone. Instead, I am to bring them to You in faith.

The story of the paralytic illustrates this so well. He had a great need. He was paralyzed and could not walk or work. He was dependent on others. Instead of his friends taking on that burden themselves, they carried him to Jesus. Literally. And when they saw there was no way to reach Jesus because of the crowds, they did not give up. Instead, in faith, they dug a hole in the roof and lowered their friend to Jesus. Seeing their faith, Jesus forgave his sins and healed him.

Lord, I ask You today to fill me with this kind of faith for the people in my life. Instead of worrying or trying to find a solution myself, empower me to bring them to You in prayer. Then, give me faith in You to know that I can trust You with the results. Show me if there is anything You want me to do for them. But most importantly, remind me to continue to bring them to You in prayer. Remove any worry from my mind today in Jesus' name. Amen.

"When Jesus returned to Capernaum several days later, the news spread quickly that he was back home. Soon the house where he was staying was so packed with visitors that there was no more room, even outside the door. While he was preaching God's word to them, four men arrived carrying a paralyzed man on a mat. They couldn't bring him to Jesus because of the crowd, so they dug a hole through the roof

above his head. Then they lowered the man on his mat, right down in front of Jesus. Seeing their faith, Jesus said to the paralyzed man, 'My child, your sins are forgiven.' But some of the teachers of religious law who were sitting there thought to themselves, 'What is he saying? This is blasphemy! Only God can forgive sins!' Jesus knew immediately what they were thinking, so he asked them, 'Why do you question this in your hearts? Is it easier to say to the paralyzed man 'Your sins are forgiven,' or 'Stand up, pick up your mat, and walk'? So I will prove to you that the Son of Man has the authority on earth to forgive sins.' Then Jesus turned to the paralyzed man and said, 'Stand up, pick up your mat, and go home!' And the man jumped up, grabbed his mat, and walked out through the stunned onlookers. They were all amazed and praised God, exclaiming, 'We've never seen anything like this before!'"

~ Mark 2:1-12 (NLT)

Story of Faith:
My Close Encounter of the God Kind
Carol Freed

I knew I should have skipped this class! "Learning to Tell Your Faith Story in Three Minutes." What an embarrassing situation this was turning into for me!

Here I was in Washington DC in 1988 at a national evangelism training conference. I did not see myself as an "evangelist," so I came to provide adult supervision of sightseeing for teens from my home church in Oregon. Besides, what "faith story" did I have?

I have no memory of not knowing about Jesus Christ as God's son and my Savior and believing the Bible to be true. My faith in God has been the foundation for my entire life. About age 7, I read the story of Solomon asking God for wisdom. That really impressed me – so I asked God: "Please give me your wisdom – if it is OK to ask for that - even though I don't expect to be as wise as Solomon!"

But asking for wisdom like Solomon probably would not qualify as the kind of "faith story" this class leader wanted. Let me think - what would be worthwhile to tell someone?

All my relatives were Lutherans, so being a believer was just the way our family lived. I liked going to church, reading my Bible and having simple conversations with God. I sang in choir and attended a Christian elementary school.

Oops, I better listen...what was he saying? Break up into pairs and practice our faith story...yuck!

What should I do now? Too late to sneak out the door! Really, why would anyone want to hear about my journey of faith?

While everyone was finding a partner, I quickly rummaged through the file cabinet of my mind looking for clues on what to say. Suddenly a friendly woman in her 30's sat down by me. Inspiration came quickly...just have her tell her story first. Maybe she will use all our time and I won't have to say anything.

Before she started, I mentally challenged God. "I'll bet she has a dramatic life-and-death kind of story, which will prove I have no story worth telling to anyone. Definitely should have skipped this class!"

Her first words were indeed dramatic. "A few years ago, I decided to kill myself." She continued: "I heard a TV preacher say, 'God loves you and you are precious to Him. He can make your life worth living.' So I asked God, if He was real, to give me the strength to get through that night. I promised to ask Jesus into my life and learn what that means." She used all our time together.

Taking on a smug attitude, I challenged God again: "See, I was right!" Hoping the class would be over soon, I was shocked when the leader told us to find a new person to practice our faith stories. This time I listened to a young man about 19. He was so on fire for God that he radiated an electric kind of energy as he talked. He had been on drugs and in a gang before becoming a Christian.

"See, God, I don't have a meaningful story. I'll be so happy to get out of this class!" I allowed him to take up all our practice time, again managing to escape sharing my insignificant "faith story."

Then it happened - like the voice of God Himself talking directly to me! The leader said: "Perhaps a few of you here are like me, receiving the blessings of being raised in a Christian family, always attending church and loving God, and feeling you have no dramatic or worthwhile story to tell anyone." By now, both God and the leader had my total attention. I could feel my heart pounding. This would be a rare opportunity to get an immediate answer from God.

The leader continued: "So what kind of faith story do we have? Our testimony is simple: 'Faith works.' We can tell people that it is possible to be raised in a Christian home, learn to love God and not go through spiritual rebellion. We can encourage people by sharing how faith is foundational to all that we do and think. We should not be ashamed of being able to explain what God's power can do, especially when it is applied to everyday life. God often uses many people to talk with a person before they become a believer. You might be a great example of a life-long Christian that a person needs to meet. The Holy Spirit will bring to you exactly the right people to hear your unique story."

I felt inspired as I realized my faith story was worthwhile after all! The Holy Spirit opened my heart to understand what I had just heard. Imagine! God cared enough about me to bring me here to learn such an important lesson. Immediately I asked God for forgiveness of my cynical comments.

My response was a simple prayer: "Dear God, I believe You revealed a new truth to me - that being raised in a Christian home is a powerful and useful faith story. I'll trust the Holy Spirit to bring to me the people who need to hear what I have experienced."

Was my prayer answered? Absolutely! Many times since then, the Holy Spirit has led me to share my story, specifically with mothers, to encourage them to model their faith in their family life because - "It works!"

My conversations with mothers have varied from a hospital bed to PTA meetings, on vacation and at conferences, but mostly in grocery stores! Nothing compares to the thrill of experiencing another close encounter of the God kind in these prearranged meetings. I am so thankful that I didn't skip that training class!

Psalm 71:17 NLT - *"Oh God, you have helped me from my earliest childhood, and I have constantly testified to others of the wonderful things you do."*

Day #16:

In order to believe someone and have faith in what they say, we need to trust them. And when it comes to how we view God, our enemy, Satan, will try to plant doubt in our minds about God's goodness towards us. We see this in the Bible even as early as Adam and Eve in the Garden when Satan said, "Did God really say...?" Genesis 3:1 (NIV)

And sometimes our view of God can become distorted. What do I mean by this? I think of it like a carnival mirror that distorts our image of ourselves. We can choose to either look in a mirror to see who we really are or in the carnival mirror to see a distorted image of ourselves. In a similar way, we can choose to look into God's Word to see who God really is or we can allow our circumstances to distort our view of God.

Let me try to explain this way. By what we believe, it is as if we are putting on a pair of glasses by which we view the world. We can put on a Biblical worldview and see our circumstances through God, or we can put on our own glasses and see God through our circumstances.

Do you see the difference?

In one scenario we are putting God first and His Word is absolute truth in our lives. In the other scenario, we are allowing our view of God to be dependent on our circumstances and the things that happen in our lives.

I remember hearing someone tell a story of growing up in a pastor's home. He said many times people in the church would complain to him about his father. And he would tell them, "You don't know my father. I know him. I live with him and I see the sacrifices he makes for the church. I see when he gets up in the middle of the night to go and pray with a family in the hospital or when he takes a phone call in the middle of dinner to be there for someone who is hurting. If you really knew my father, you wouldn't say these things about him."

And I wonder how well we know our heavenly Father. Because when we know Him so well through His Word, then we will know that He is good. No matter what happens in our lives, we will be able to say, "I know my Father and I know that He is good. Even though I don't understand, I can trust Him."

How well do you know your heavenly Father today? In order to believe in Him and have faith in Him, you need to be able to trust Him and know that He is good, that He is a good God.

"Suffering provides the gym equipment on which my faith can be exercised."
~ Joni Eareckson Tada

"God's plan and His ways of working out His plan are frequently beyond our ability to fathom and understand. We must learn to trust when we don't understand."
~ Jerry Bridge

"If you look at the world, you'll be distressed. If you look within, you'll be depressed. If you look at God you'll be at rest."
~Corrie ten Boom

The Faith Challenge:

➤ Have there been circumstances in your life which have distorted your view of God? Or can you say confidently today, "I know my Father! And He is good." One way to get to know your heavenly Father is through His Word. For more resources to help you develop a healthy view of God, go to http://discovergod.com/character

➤ I experienced a difficult season in my life where my view of God became distorted. God gave me three pictures that helped me rebuild my faith and trust in Him that I share in my eBook, "Trusting God When Bad Things Happen." You can also listen as I share my journey and what God taught me via video or audio here: www.christianspeakers.tv/when-bad-things-happen.

Prayer of Faith:
Jesus' Obedience

Lord, I am so thankful for the example You have given us in Jesus. He had ultimate trust in You and faith in Your plan even when it was not what His flesh wanted. Faith leads to obedience. And I see this lived out so clearly in the life of Christ. He said He did nothing by Himself but only what He saw You, His Father, doing.

Therefore, I not only need to have faith in You but to also prove my faith in You through my obedience to Your commands. And I do not have to do this in my own strength or my own sufficiency. I can do all things through Christ who strengthens me.

Empower me to obey You even when it is difficult and hard. Help me to follow the example Christ set for me when He walked this earth. I love You so much, Lord. Amen.

"Jesus gave them this answer: 'Very truly I tell you, the Son can do nothing by himself; he can do only what he sees his Father doing, because whatever the Father does the Son also does.'"

~John 5:19 (NIV)

"I can do all things through him who strengthens me."

~ Philippians 4:13 (ESV)

Story of Faith:
The Cupbearer
Laura J. Marshall

Like dirty fingerprints on a clear glass, so is the animosity that comes from someone in great opposition to God. The cup hovers over me, a reminder, as if the enemy whispers, "This one's mine." And I pray.

I am a cupbearer.

The smudged cups stack up. They cling to my mind in their emptiness.

Faith sees the potential.

Faith sees the need.

115

Faith sees the water that washes.

I am a cupbearer.

Sometimes I am afraid to see all the cups and carry them. Yet, I balance them in patience and gaze on them in forbearance and prayer.

I bear the cups to the feet of the Lord. He looks on them with compassion and love, tears filling His eyes, "It is for these I came into the world."

I can't help but spill a bit of the Lord's overflowing mercy as I walk.

I am a cupbearer.

I bear the cups with me as I go on my way. As my days increase, I carry more. Their weight can become heavy.

Returning to His feet, I lift each one. He nods. Their burden becomes light. These I bear all my life with my life.

I am a cupbearer.

My prayers will be everlasting. For only God knows if a cup has been cleansed. I am just a cupbearer. I am not brave. Faith is brave. Valiant. Faith bears the cups.

Faith holds them close, closer still and looks on each with the ministrations of hope and confidence.

I am a cupbearer.

I am faith.

~~~~~~

Faith is active and has substance.

The longer I travel through this life, the more I collect faces of wrath, words, voices, gestures. Repeatedly they visit on the wings of the Holy Spirit. Some are more painful than others to look upon. Most didn't know I existed, but I saw, heard, or felt their presence. I've tried to protect my eyes and ears, weighing my steps and where I tread, yet our paths cross and I often wonder if it isn't divined by God. Through our faith, we all are cupbearers…carrying others in prayer to the feet of the Lord. Faith is modest, industrious, courageous, and confident. It has great influence. As I ponder the picture God gave me, I wonder why I wasn't carrying cups of wrath. The cups were empty, smudged and dirty. Do I carry the cups of my children to the feet of the Lord? Are they colorful and with fingerprints? Are they empty vessels or full?

Day #17:

God is teaching me that living a life of faith often means looking beyond what I can see with my human eyes. It can be easy to look at my life circumstances and jump to conclusions. However, things may not always be as they appear.

I encourage you to go back and read the story of Joseph in Genesis. It is a powerful story of God using the difficult times in Joseph's life for good. His brothers sold him into slavery. He ended up in Egypt and through a course of circumstances, he was put in charge of a project that would literally save those in Egypt and the surrounding countries, including Joseph's family, from starvation.

Joseph told his brothers who sold him into slavery, *"You intended to harm me, but God intended it for good to accomplish what is now being done, the saving of many lives."* Genesis 50:20 (NIV)

I can now see how God is using the painful experiences in my past for good. The enemy meant to harm and destroy me, but God is using it for good. And He wants to do the same in your life.

This poem describes it so well...

"The Weaver"
~Anonymous

> *My life is but a weaving, between my God and me,*
> *I do not choose the colors, He worketh steadily,*

118

Oftimes He weaveth sorrow, and I in foolish pride,
Forget He sees the upper, and I the underside.
Not till the loom is silent, and shuttles cease to fly,
Will God unroll the canvas and explain the reason
why.
The dark threads are as needful in the skillful
Weaver's hand,
As the threads of gold and silver in the pattern He has
planned.

The Faith Challenge:

❖ Have you seen God bring good out of difficult times in your life? Write your answer to this question in a journal or discuss it with a friend.

❖ I encourage you to declare your trust in God through prayer. Feel free to use the prayer I have written out below or to pray a prayer from your heart.

Lord, I realize that I may never have all the answers to my questions this side of heaven. But, I ask that You continue to reveal Yourself to me, giving me wisdom and understanding. Help me to trust You with the things I still don't understand.

I thank You that You have promised to walk through every painful trial with me. That You will never leave me or forsake me. I thank You that even when other people fail me, You will never fail me. Help me to put my faith and trust in You and not in people or circumstances. I thank You that even if I can't see it, You promise to bring good out of the pain in my life (Romans 8:28). I love You, I worship You, I trust You. Amen.

Prayer of Faith:
Salvation

Lord, today I want to thank You for my salvation. I know that without You, I would have no hope beyond this life. For I have sinned against You in so many ways and my sin separates me from You. Thank You that You have given me the gift of eternal life through the sacrifice Jesus made on the cross. So many misunderstand You...You did not send Jesus to condemn the world, but to save it. I pray that my unsaved relatives and friends would come to truly know You and trust in Jesus for their salvation. For when we confess with our mouths that Jesus is Lord and believe in our hearts that You raised him from the dead, we will be saved.

I thank You that salvation is truly a gift from You, nothing I can earn by doing good works or trying harder. Faith without works is dead, but ultimately salvation comes only as a gift from You.

I praise You that I am a new creation – the old has passed away and the new has come. Thank You for changing my heart and my life...I am forever grateful to You. Help me to share my relationship with You with others. Amen.

"For all have sinned and fall short of the glory of God."
~ Romans 3:23 (NKJV)

"For the wages of sin is death, but the gift of God is eternal life in Christ Jesus our Lord."
~ Romans 6:23 (NKJV)

"For God so loved the world that He gave His only begotten Son, that whoever believes in Him should not perish but have

*everlasting life. For God did not send His Son into the world
to condemn the world, but that the world through Him might
be saved."*

~ John 3:16-17 (NKJV)

*"That if you confess with your mouth the Lord Jesus and
believe in your heart that God has raised Him from the dead,
you will be saved."*

~ Romans 10:9 (NKJV)

*"For by grace you have been saved through faith, and that not
of yourselves; it is the gift of God."*

~ Ephesians 2:8 (NKJV)

"Thus also faith by itself, if it does not have works, is dead."

~ James 2:17 (NKJV)

*"Therefore, if anyone is in Christ, he is a new creation; old
things have passed away; behold, all things have become
new."*

~ 2 Corinthians 5:17 (NKJV)

Story of Faith:
Learning to Stand

Cheryl Rogers

"The Lord shall fight for you, and ye shall hold your peace."

~ Exodus 14:14 KJV

Prayer is powerful.

When I succumbed to a severe immune disorder many years
ago, I learned just how powerful. After seeking prayer
wherever and whenever I could, God restored my life to me.
But now He has brought me to a new place in my faith walk.

I had become accustomed to storming heaven with prayer requests for myself and my loved ones. I'd become accustomed to calling on the intercessors, praying and fasting when I could. Now God whispers: Hold your peace and watch Me work for you. I ask myself – Do I really need to try and convince Him? Am I praying for something He doesn't want too? Am I praying for something He has already done? Because I am praying the promises He has made in His Word, I know the answers.

We are spiritual creatures. What we see manifested in the flesh happens first in the spirit realm. So when I was healed many years ago, the healing initially occurred when the Holy Spirit came to indwell me. That was the real healing. I became a true child of God, gifted and called for His purposes on Earth. No longer alone, powerless against the enemy. No longer spiritually bruised and battered, because HE came into my life.

He also quickened my mortal body by His Spirit (Romans 8:11). It took a while for that to manifest in my body weakened by a disease doctors were powerless to defeat. But it wasn't too much for God, the One who made me and who knew how to fix me. It wasn't too much for the God that crafted our bodies fearfully and wonderfully (Psalm 139:14), enabling them to heal themselves if they are given the proper fuel and rest.

Through that experience, I learned to depend upon God, not man. I learned He's made our bodies resilient and with an incredible capacity for abuse. We're assaulted by toxins, food additives and stress. Our food is denatured and stripped of the nutrients God has placed there for us. We whip up concoctions that taste great but do little but add inches to our waistlines. In the end, we can't top what He's already given us.

I learned to rely on God for the answers to my questions and solutions to my problems. Although my natural inclination is to peruse the Internet for answers, at times I let Him quiet this urging. Deep inside, I know He already has the answers. Deep inside, I know He is with me and for me (Hebrews 13:5). And I know I can't trust myself to sort lies from truth.

And so, in this new place, I realize God is calling on me to trust Him, to recognize I must wait for His plan to unfold. Instead of letting panic reign, He has called me to a faith that does indeed move mountains rather than quake in fear.

The gentle whispering of the Holy Spirit comforts me, assuring me of His presence and of His faithfulness. He whispers that He desires to answer my prayers right now, but lets me know it's not the best plan.

He is showing me when we can't change others or our circumstances, we can still change ourselves.

And so I have a choice. I can focus on the good things, make the most of what I have, pray unceasingly for Him to make good on the promises in His word, and stand in faith. Or I can give in to self-pity, doubt and misery. I can focus on the problems and feel overwhelmed. I can give up.

I love prayer intercessors. I intercede for others. But in this new place, I recognize He is my all. He is my Alpha and Omega (Revelation 1:11). I can stand in faith.

I'm still praying. I know we need to pray unceasingly (1 Thessalonians 5:17). I know we must resist the enemy so he will flee (James 4:7). I know our weapons are spiritual, not carnal (2 Corinthians 10:4). But my yoke is easy (Matthew 11:30) because I'm not taking on the weight of that responsibility. He has made and He will bear (Isaiah 46:4).

He intercedes for me (Romans 8:26).

Day #18:

Many times faith cannot be figured out, reasoned or analyzed. God does want us to use our intellect and the minds He has given us. But sometimes, when He asks us to do something in faith, it may not make sense in our human minds.

Simon Peter experienced this with Jesus in Luke 5:4-6. *"When He (Jesus) had stopped speaking, He said to Simon, 'Launch out into the deep and let down your nets for a catch.' But Simon answered and said to Him, 'Master, we have toiled all night and caught nothing; nevertheless at Your word I will let down the net.' And when they had done this, they caught a great number of fish, and their net was breaking."* (NKJV)

Simon Peter was a fisherman by trade and knew the ins and outs of fishing. He had been fishing all night and did not catch even one fish. It did not make sense to go back out and put his nets in the water again. However, did you see his response to Jesus?

Nevertheless at Your word, I will obey.

Nevertheless.

In saying this, Simon Peter was saying that he was choosing to submit to Christ instead of submitting to his own intellect and reasoning. We see a similar response from Jesus in the garden of Gethsemane prior to his death on the cross. He says, *"O My Father, if it is possible, let this cup pass from Me; nevertheless, not as I will, but as You will."* (NKJV)

Nevertheless.

How will you respond to God today?

"The man that believes will obey; failure to obey is convincing proof that there is no true faith present. To attempt the impossible God must give faith or there will be none, and He gives faith to the obedient heart only."

~ A. W. Tozer

"God is God. Because He is God, He is worthy of my trust and obedience. I will find rest nowhere but in His holy will, a will that is unspeakably beyond my largest notions of what He is up to."

~ Elisabeth Elliot

"God's commands are designed to guide you to life's very best. You will not obey Him, if you do not believe Him and trust Him. You cannot believe Him if you do not love Him. You cannot love Him unless you know Him."

~ Henry Blackaby

The Faith Challenge:

➢ Even when it does not make sense or "add up" in your mind, are you willing to obey God and say "nevertheless"? Write out your response in your journal or discuss it with a friend.

Prayer of Faith:
Love

Lord, I thank You that my relationship with You is not built around rules but instead is built upon love. Sometimes I get into a pattern of simply coming to you out of routine and habit. I do know that creating a habit of meeting with you is important. However, what is even more important is that my heart connects with you on a regular basis.

I can have all the faith in the world and yet if I do not have love, my faith means nothing. Therefore, today I ask You to fill me to overflowing with Your love. If there is any part of my heart that has become cold, I ask You to fill it with Your love once again. Show me Lord if there is anything blocking me from truly living a life of love. Reveal to me any unforgiveness, resentment, bitterness or hate in my heart. Right now, I confess that my heart has grown cold in this area _____ (fill in the blank). Please forgive me and wash me clean through Your forgiveness. Fill me once again with Your spirit and Your love. Thank you Lord. Amen.

"If I speak in the tongues of men and of angels, but have not love, I am a noisy gong or a clanging cymbal. And if I have prophetic powers, and understand all mysteries and all knowledge, and if I have all faith, so as to remove mountains, but have not love, I am nothing. If I give away all I have, and if I deliver up my body to be burned, but have not love, I gain nothing."

~ I Corinthians 13:1-3 (ESV)

Story of Faith:
A New Beginning

Carol McCormick

I came into this world during a time when traditional family life and values were the norm, but grew up with the fads and the standards of the 60's and 70's.

During my teenage years, I didn't have much interest in spiritual things, other than an occasional prayer before bed. I often skipped religious instruction classes to go downtown and sit on the benches in front of city hall, to smoke cigarettes and watch boys go by. The Vietnam War was in full swing, as were student, political, prison, and race riots. The 70's brought a revolution, and with it, turbulence and a change in American culture and its values.

Enticed by the lure of pleasure, excitement, and the illusion of invincibility, I was caught up in a wave of rebellion, and engaged in many of the typical activities that were prevalent during the 70's hippie movement. Most of my friends were written up in the newspaper on a regular basis for breaking the law in one form or another, which led to my own lax attitude about authority.

When I turned eighteen, I moved out of the house and finished my last month of high school while living at friends' homes. Immediately after graduation, I began working as a hairstylist in a beauty salon where I found a loving family atmosphere that gave a sense of security and order to my life, although there was still something missing. A void existed in my heart that I could not fill with drinking, partying, or making money. I had no power to change my circumstances which were spiraling downhill fast, and I thought, is this all there is? There must be something more.

The following Christmas, I asked for and received a Bible as a gift. I opened it to the book of Genesis and read the Creation story, but I couldn't relate to anything there, so I turned to the New Testament and read the genealogies. I couldn't relate to anything there either, so I opened to the book of Proverbs where I found the seven things that the Lord hates. I could relate to some of those things, since I was doing them, so I closed the Bible, thinking that there was no hope for me and went further from the Lord for three more years.

Then one day while visiting my aunt, I found a book in her home about survival. Thinking it was about camping in the wilderness, I happily took it home. To my surprise, it was actually about the book of Revelation. The book opened up a whole new world to me that I had never heard about before. It said things like people would vanish in the "twinkling of an eye" and judgment would befall those left behind. I also noticed little words and numbers under these statements and somehow I knew they were Scriptures, so I looked them up. I was shocked to find that these strange quotes were really in the Bible, and I got scared. I knew that I would be in big trouble if these events occurred during my lifetime, so I started searching for answers.

It happened that around this time, my employer became a Christian. While working together, I asked her questions about her newfound faith, and after we had talked awhile, she said, "I know you're going to become a Christian, because you have the desire." But in my mind, I thought, "I wish it were true," but you really don't know me.

Shortly after this time, I heard a minister's wife speak about her rebellious past, and I suddenly felt there was hope for me in my own lost condition. As this woman described her wayward ways, I felt as though she was describing my life.

When she quoted the Bible and said, "All have sinned and come short of the glory of God," and, "All we like sheep have gone astray, we have turned every one to his own way," I felt as though she was speaking to me. She said that Jesus bore all of our sins when He died on the cross and rose again, and then she proceeded to tell the audience that she was going to Heaven someday.

How could she say such a thing?!

I stayed behind to question this woman who made such a bold proclamation. I wanted to know, because deep in my heart, I wanted to go there too. She explained the way of salvation again in a sweet and loving tone, and I told her that I wanted to become a Christian, but I couldn't stop sinning. She showed me from the Bible that it is by grace that we are saved through faith, and that it was a gift from God. She asked me again if I would like to pray, and I said, "Not yet! I can't stop sinning!" I thought I had to be good first, before I came to Christ.

We went back-and-forth like this for three more times until she patiently showed me the verse that said, "Not by works of righteousness which we have done, but according to his mercy He saved us." I finally understood that God loved me right where I was and that Jesus died for all of my sins. I was ready to stop going my own way and surrender my life to Christ. She led me in a prayer that changed my life as I asked for forgiveness and asked Jesus to come into my heart and save me. At that moment, I felt clean inside. A huge burden seemed to have been lifted from my shoulders, and I had a new beginning. I was free! I was forgiven! And by the grace of God, I was going to Heaven!

Day #19:

Congratulations on making it to day 19 in this faith challenge. I pray that your faith has been strengthened and is growing each day through the empowerment of Christ. However, I wanted to take time today to remind all of us that even *"if I have a faith that can move mountains, but do not have love, I am nothing."* I Corinthians 13:2b (NIV)

Faith – Love = Nothing

"And now these three remain: faith, hope and love. But the greatest of these is love."

~ I Corinthians 13:13 (NIV)

"'Teacher, which is the greatest commandment in the Law?' Jesus replied: 'Love the Lord your God with all your heart and with all your soul and with all your mind. This is the first and greatest commandment. And the second is like it: Love your neighbor as yourself. All the Law and the Prophets hang on these two commandments.'"

~ Matthew 22: 36-40 (NIV)

"Spread the love of God through your life but only use words when necessary."

~Mother Teresa

"I'm a little pencil in the hand of a writing God, who is sending a love letter to the world."

~ Mother Teresa

The Faith Challenge:

> ➤ And the greatest of these is love. Ask God to fill you with His love today. Without love, your faith will mean nothing.

Prayer of Faith:
Faith and Works

Father, thank You for the ways You are growing my faith in You. I know that on this side of heaven, I will continue to have opportunities to trust You and put my faith in You.

However, Your Word tells me that faith without works is dead. In fact, even the demons believe in You and shudder. And so I want my faith in You to be more than just a belief in You. I want my faith to result in obedience to You. Help me to not only talk to You in my prayers, but to also take the time to listen to You. You speak to me clearly through Your Word and through Your Holy Spirit.

Thank You, Lord, that Your Word is a lamp unto my feet and a light unto my path. Empower me to follow You in obedience as You lead me each day. Thank You for Your Presence that is with me every day. In Jesus' name I pray, Amen.

"What does it profit, my brethren, if someone says he has faith but does not have works? Can faith save him? If a brother or sister is naked and destitute of daily food, and one of you says to them, 'Depart in peace, be warmed and filled,' but you do not give them the things which are needed for the body, what does it profit? Thus also faith by itself, if it does not have works, is dead."

~ James 2:14-17 (NKJV)

"You believe that God is one; you do well. Even the demons believe—and shudder!"

~James 2:19 (ESV)

"Your word is a lamp to my feet and a light to my path."

~ Psalm 119:105 (ESV)

Story of Faith:
Faith Like a Mustard Seed
Victor Brodt

Luke 17:1-10

"I have seen many cases like this before; she fits all the profiles." The doctor quickly spoke as he flashed various tests and charts before my gaze. The papers flew by too quickly for even the most trained eye. He was a busy person, most often the last in the line of experts. He seemed to carry the weight of a man hounded by the masses to fix what no one else could solve.

"She may have 6 months to live," the doctor pronounced pointedly.

There in the busy hospital hallway, a nurse's station buzzed and whirled, but for me time slowly froze and the noise faded.

133

The walls grew close as if the whole world was shrinking. Life would get even harder. His quick, curt speech was supposed to prepare me to lose the love of my life.

I thought that I had already done one of the hardest things in life, I had left my pastorate. It was a wonderful growing church, the attendance had doubled in short order; it was my dream come true; interrupted by a nightmare. We found that I needed to leave behind my plans, my hopes, and my dreams in order to care for my beloved bride as she went through surgeries and mysterious afflictions.

There in the hospital hallway, I stared at the stark green walls; it seemed only moments before when my wife and I had gazed at another view; it was a time when we knew very little about things religious. We were on our honeymoon touring Europe. We took in all of the artwork we could; there was one stop on the highly recommended list, a church called Sacred Heart. There we stood looking up at something like the unfathomable expanse of the Grand Canyon, but this was man-made. The huge dome contained a ceramic mosaic designed to last to the end of time. It seemed to me a perfect artistry. The tiles made up the largest of paintings, and one subject surrounded you, and lovingly looked into your eyes. There he was, arms wide open; it was Jesus. We felt as if we had met him for the first time, as if we could now see His love. The artist had captured the impossible. Perhaps this would be exactly like our first glimpse of real heaven.

There in the hospital hallway, I wanted us to just be in His arms. I wished my wife and I could simply go to Him, now, together...

After Sacred Heart we continued our tour of Europe, but shortly we made a distinction. There were churches, and then there were Jesus churches; some were centered on relics and material things. Some were centered on Jesus, and seemed to exude His love and wonder. In a hotel in Florence, Italy, my beautiful bride, a Jewish lady, did, what we thought at the time, no one like her in 2000 years had done. She prayed to receive Jesus. The decision was not a casual or easy one for either of us.

When we returned to the US we were amazed to find others like us who had found the real Jesus. Life became unusual; together we were baptized in the ocean. On Malibu beach, a sunbathing Jane Fonda was an unwitting witness. Not long afterward we toured the world with an evangelistic group. My wife and I were firebrands, and we experienced what often seemed just like living chapters in the book of Acts. Surely God was with us. Then there was seminary, a son, and finally finding the place I felt I belonged even before I had become a Christian; the pastorate. Life was very good, and then suddenly came the nightmare.

The Wall of Pain

Pain demands your attention, severe pain may be numbed with drugs or other means, but when it refuses to relent it becomes unbearable. When hope fades, it gets even worse. We did not know the real future but the doctor was wrong; she lived and we struggled on. Many voices told us to give up. Often I told her I felt her pain; little did we realize that we actually shared the same affliction; hers was much further along, but I was busy doing the best I could to care for her.

When we were first married, we thought there could be no couple that could love each other more, but there really is much, much more to real love. The struggle taught us more than we could have imagined. When there is serious long term suffering it comes down to a decision, a decision to love, a decision to face the impossible, and a decision to forgive and resolve. There are many ways to cut and run, but Christian or not there is a kind of decision that really is faith being worked out.

I started a new business that was flexible for my wife's care and somehow with God's help we managed to be very successful; this allowed us to try every medical option imaginable but it is clear to me that it was really faith that held us together. Ultimately behind my story is a common secret that keeps many of us from utter ruin; it is our God given tendency to apply faith to even the most difficult of situations.

When it comes to the things of the Bible I am very well educated. I learned Greek and Hebrew. I studied under some of the best scholars. Truthfully faith is gigantic and beyond comprehension. I understand faith somewhat; but you should know that faith is a concept that humbles all mortals. We often fail and flail. Faith could feel weak, even when it may be very strong. If you think of faith like building a muscle you will get confused; you are not a 90 lb. weakling that just needs to try harder. It is a self-defeating lie to feel guilty because you have not exercised enough faith. It might be best to think of faith as a fragile gift, a gift you cannot buy from others, or earn. The gift awaits you but there are some things to understand, some things which hinder and some that help.

Faith is not ignoring reality and trying to believe something that is not true. It is not a pull yourself up by your boot straps attitude. In the Biblical sense it is not simply a positive attitude or the mindset that everything will go your way; this is really an old distorted view that comes from man and it is not God's manner.

Faith is increased by absorbing God's word so fully, that you listen and do what it says in spite of what other voices say. Faith is evidenced by applying God's principles. Biblical

136

giving and serving will allow your faith to grow, but choosing to worry and fear will eat away at your soul and you will be misled into feeling like you have no faith at all. Unforgiveness and bitterness will most likely make your faith feel as powerless as Samson after a haircut. This should never be.

Over twenty-five years ago, the doctor gave my wife 6 months to live. I wonder if he is still alive? My wife is. Life has not been easy, nor has it gone as planned; in fact it has been an impossible journey. In the midst of all this, love, respect, and admiration have grown deep and enormously strong. Faith has somehow turned the pain into something precious like gold; eternal gold. We have often felt weak, but after all this time I also know there is something very strong; it is very much like a mustard seed, and it is also very much like a great and strong tree planted by deep waters.

Day #20:

Several enemies to faith are doubt, worry, and fear. Many times they are planted in our minds through the lies of the enemy. The Bible tells us that our enemy, Satan, is the father of all lies and that there is no truth in him.

"You belong to your father, the devil, and you want to carry out your father's desires. He was a murderer from the beginning, not holding to the truth, for there is no truth in him. When he lies, he speaks his native language, for he is a liar and the father of lies."

~ John 8:44 (NIV)

What might these lies look like? In the past I have taken the time to not only write out the lies that I believed, but also to write out the truth of what God says about it from Scripture. I then write the truth on a notecard and carry it around with me. Sometimes I have needed to re-read the truth card multiple times throughout the day to fight the battle waging within my mind.

Here are two examples:

Lie: I cannot trust God because He has let me down in the past.

Truth: God is faithful and has my best interests in mind, even when I can't understand His ways. He will help me begin to trust Him again. He wants me to trust Him and I want to trust Him. (Lamentations 3:5-6; Isaiah 55:9; Proverbs 3:5-6; Psalm 91:1-3)

Lie: I am afraid of what the future holds.

Truth: God has plans for me - to prosper me and not to harm me, to give me a hope and a future. I can trust Him with my future. He is walking before me, preparing the way. (Jeremiah 29:11; Isaiah 43:18-19)

Practical Steps to Overcoming Lies with God's Truth

I want to share some practical steps God has used in my life to help me replace the lies of the enemy with God's truth.

Step#1: Recognize the lies. *John 10:10*

Step #2: Take your stand in the spiritual battle. Command Satan and his demons to leave in the authority of Jesus' name. When you resist the devil, he will flee from you. *Ephesians 6:10-18, James 4:7*

Step #3: Uproot the lie by confessing your sin of believing the lie (and any other sin you acted on because of the lie). *I John 1:9*

Step #4: Repent, asking for God's forgiveness for living your life based upon the lie. *Luke 5:32*

Step #5: Replace the lie with God's truth. Invite Jesus to come and the Holy Spirit to fill you with His truth (the opposite of the lie). *John 8:32*

"We're going to have to let truth scream louder to our souls than the lies that have infected us."

~ Beth Moore

The Faith Challenge:

> ➤ I encourage you to come up with your own truth cards. Search the scriptures using tools like www.BibleGateway.com, www.YouVersion.com or www.BlueLetterBible.org to find scriptures that relate to what you are going through. Re-word them into truths that you can carry with you and repeat until they replace the lies you have been believing!

Prayer of Faith:
God's Word

Lord, thank You for Your Word, the Bible. Through it, You speak to me, teach me, and help me to grow in my relationship with You. Strengthen my faith in Your Word today. May You help me to believe that Your Word is absolute truth. It is alive and full of power and applicable to my life today.

All Scripture has been inspired by You and I can put my trust in it. Give me a hunger and thirst for Your Word. May I see it as life-giving and necessary for my spiritual life. May Your Holy Spirit teach me through Your Word and help me to understand it and apply it to my life. I love you! Amen.

"For the Word that God speaks is alive and full of power [making it active, operative, energizing, and effective]; it is sharper than any two-edged sword, penetrating to the dividing line of the breath of life (soul) and [the immortal] spirit, and of joints and marrow [of the deepest parts of our nature], exposing and sifting and analyzing and judging the very thoughts and purposes of the heart."

~ Hebrews 4:12 (AMP)

"Every Scripture is God-breathed (given by His inspiration) and profitable for instruction, for reproof and conviction of sin, for correction of error and discipline in obedience, [and] for training in righteousness (in holy living, in conformity to God's will in thought, purpose, and action)."

~ 2 Timothy 3:16 (AMP)

Story of Faith:
Releasing Divine Faith

Rev. Paul B. Heidt

God made magnificent promises to each of us in his Word— the sixty-six books of the Bible. They are not dead words as so many people believe. No, they are alive as much now as ever before. How do you identify what God is saying to you through His Word and have enough faith to see it come to pass in your life? The steps for how to do that are clear when we see how the faith of a leader named Joshua worked to accomplish God's plan for his life.

God promised Joshua that he would lead the children of Israel into the Promised Land of Israel. That meant leading two million Hebrews over a flooded river, commanding thousands of soldiers to clear the land of its pagan beliefs and, ultimately, taking possession of its villages. Why did Joshua attempt such an enormous task? Perhaps the primary reason is that God gave him a promise that He would be with Joshua throughout the process, never leaving him or forsaking him, just as He was with Moses.

Foreseeing the obstacles and struggles that awaited him, it took Joshua great courage and great faith to take the reins of Moses and move God's children into their promised possession. Joshua's faith didn't rely on the tradition and rules

given to Moses nor did Joshua sit back and make faith a god—
expecting God's promise to come into being without any
effort on his part. Joshua knew that he needed a divine faith
that would bring him victory—a faith that is available to each
of us.

Behind every great accomplishment for God is a great season
of preparation. This was true for Joshua—God's leader and
general over Israel who led two million plus Hebrews into
their promised land. We get a hint of his preparation in Joshua
1:1:

*"Now after the death of Moses, the servant of the Lord it came
to pass that the Lord spoke to Joshua, the son of Nun, Moses'
minister."* (NKJV- emphasis mine).

The word "minister" is significant because it can also be
translated "disciple," "servant," or "aid." I like the word
"servant." This is a critical concept to grasp because genuine
faith that prepares to possess God's promises always begins
with servanthood. Joshua lived a servant life as he built his
faith and pursued God's plan for his life, and so can you.

Possess a Servant's Heart

Have you felt called into the five-fold ministry—apostle,
prophet, evangelist, pastor, or teacher? Or do you think you've
been anointed to succeed as a business person, nurse,
contractor, or other occupation? Whichever path God leads
you into, it doesn't begin on the platform of a church or
behind a desk in an executive suite. It begins by being
somebody else's aid—following somebody else around,
setting up chairs, washing someone's car and doing someone
else's errands with a servant's attitude.

Why is being a servant such an important aspect of faith? It's simple. If you cannot obey and serve someone you can see, will you really be able to obey and serve God whom you cannot?

Rick Renner, a great Bible teacher and author, said that while he was preparing for ministry, a prominent pastor asked him to shine his alligator shoes. How would you have felt about that request? Grateful? Ready to shine? Rick did his duty, albeit grudgingly. Fortunately, he learned the principle of servanthood over time, and it has produced much fruit in his ministry today.

I remember a guest speaker who came to my church a long time ago. After a three-hour service wearing three-inch high heels, she and her disciple came to my house. The speaker sat on my sofa and took off her shoes. What do you think her aid did? Without even being asked, she walked up to the speaker and proceeded to massage her feet. I said to myself, now there's a servant!

Remember: a faith that won't willingly submit in serving others is a faith that won't be released to accomplish God's plan.

Some of the most important days in my ministry preparation involved learning how to submit to men and women of God in the church, at Bible College, and in seminary. I remember the night that no one wanted to help a well-known evangelist at his resource table during a conference at Zion Bible College. Everyone wanted to be in the service to see what God was doing, including me. Yet, something prompted me to help the evangelist in the exhibit hall. So I did. At the last second, he changed his mind and decided to set up his table in the gym where the service was in progress. I learned the importance of being a servant when no one else wanted to be, and I was rewarded for it. I received a double blessing: I enjoyed the service and was blessed to assist the man of God at his resource table.

Invariably, choosing to serve someone at your own expense is not easy. It doesn't always result in a blessing either, at least not right away. Nevertheless, if you want a faith that possesses God's plan for your life, it begins by being a servant now, a minister now, someone's aid now.

You might say, "I've never heard that serving others is a part of faith." That's why so few people actually walk by faith or manifest great faith! Too many people in the church would rather listen to messages about faith than release it through true servanthood. Paul discussed this problem in his letter to the Philippians:

"I trust in the Lord Jesus to send Timothy to you shortly, that I also may be encouraged when I know your state. For I have no one like-minded, who will sincerely care for your state. For all seek their own, not the things which are of Christ Jesus. But you know his proven character, that as a son with his father he served with me in the gospel." (Philippians 2:19-22, NKJV- emphasis mine).

Timothy served Paul. Paul served Barnabas. The disciples served Christ. Elisha served Elijah. And Joshua served Moses. Serving others is an important dynamic of releasing divine faith. It prepares you for possessing God's plan, and you will never possess it without grasping how faith works through servanthood.

Day #21:

It is hard to believe that today is the final day of this faith challenge. In closing, let's look at two obstacles to faith: unbelief and pride. We see both of these obstacles described in Luke chapter 9.

In the beginning of the chapter it tells us that Jesus gave His twelve disciples *"power and authority to drive out all demons and to cure diseases, and He sent them out to proclaim the kingdom of God and to heal the sick."* Luke 9:1-2 (NIV)

Later in the chapter the disciples attempted to cast out a demon from one man's son. However, it says "they could not." (Luke 9:40). If they were given power and authority to drive out ALL demons, where did the power go?

Matthew 17:19-20 tells us what happened to their power. It was replaced with unbelief. *"Then the disciples came to Jesus in private and asked, 'Why couldn't we drive it out?' He replied, 'Because you have so little faith. Truly I tell you, if you have faith as small as a mustard seed, you can say to this mountain, move from here to there, and it will move. Nothing will be impossible for you.'"*

In Luke 9:41 Jesus addresses the disciples this way, *"You unbelieving and perverse generation."* (NIV)

How do you think the disciples were feeling after this evident failure on their part? What do you think they would be talking about? Amazingly enough, "an argument started among the disciples as to which of them would be the greatest." Luke

9:46 (NIV) Instead of being humbled, they were talking about who was the greatest. Most likely, pride entered their hearts and replaced the power of God in their lives.

As you continue this life of faith, beware of these two obstacles: unbelief and pride. Any time you recognize these obstacles, confess your sin, repent, and then ask for God's empowerment through His Holy Spirit to truly live out a life of faith.

I pray that Jesus says to you, *"According to your faith let it be done to you."* Matthew 9:29 (NIV)

"For with God nothing will be impossible."
~ Luke 1:37 (NKJV)

The Faith Challenge:

> ➤ How has God been working in your life throughout this 21 days of faith challenge? Write out your own story of faith in your journal, share what God has been doing in your life with a friend or share your faith stories in our private Facebook group here: www.facebook.com/groups/21daysoffaith.

Prayer of Faith:
Pleasing God

Lord, I want to please You with my life. I know that Your Word says that without faith it is impossible to please You. Therefore, I desire to continue to grow in my faith in You each day. My faith is similar to a muscle. The more I use it, the more it grows. However, I am so thankful that it is not up to me to increase my faith. I am so thankful that You are the author and the perfecter of my faith. When my faith feels weak or wavers, I simply need to come to You and ask You for help.

Thank You for all that You are doing in my life, Lord. Help me to keep my eyes fixed on You and not on my circumstances or on myself. I love you so much. In Jesus' name I pray, Amen.

"And without faith it is impossible to please God, because anyone who comes to him must believe that he exists and that he rewards those who earnestly seek him."
                                                    ~ Hebrews 11:6 (NIV)

"Therefore, since we are surrounded by so great a cloud of witnesses, let us also lay aside every weight, and sin which clings so closely, and let us run with endurance the race that is set before us, looking to Jesus, the founder and perfecter of our faith, who for the joy that was set before him endured the cross, despising the shame, and is seated at the right hand of the throne of God."
                                                    ~ Hebrews 12:1-2 (ESV)

Story of Faith:
When Motives Are Rewarded
Marilynn Dawson

My faith story seems to be a never-ending series of adventures. I entered another one at the end of January 2013.

That day, my boss sat me down in his office and nearly broke into tears twice as he shared that due to lack of work he'd have to let me go. The news hurt, but he was the one needing a hug when it was over. He is a fellow believer and attends a local Mennonite church with his family.

That night I was tempted to get concerned about the future, 'til I realized God had just answered my prayer for time to make two changes in my current lifestyle. One change was to add time for walks. Walking is my favorite form of exercise and I haven't been able to do it as much as I used to. The other was to regain uninterrupted quiet time with just me and the unseen Lover of my soul. Sure it's good to have conversational prayer off and on throughout the day, to open the Scriptures to answer someone. But I wanted that quiet private time too. As a single working mother, that isn't an easy thing to schedule on a regular basis due to life changing every 3 to 6 months whether I need it to or not. So there I was that evening, realizing that suddenly I could call my own hours again! I could put these two desires into action finally!

I began my quiet times reviewing a devotional on Genesis by Nicole Vaughn. The first week I had two days of self-employed work. I had devotions every morning and only missed one day's walk. The second week there was hardly any self-employed work, but again, only really missed one day's walk. Then February 18th arrived!

A realtor my former boss knows from the local Rotary club called wanting to hire someone, as work for him is getting busy and he needed assistance in the office. He asked if I'd come for an interview at 7pm that night. I'm not really sold on the idea of secretarial work, but as it was a referral from my former boss, I couldn't say no and went for what would be a very casual, unstructured, "help me while we talk" interview that I got paid for! I assisted him for two hours as we talked about what I was expecting, the wage, the hours I was hoping to engage in to implement desired changes in my life, etc. This realtor accommodated without much hassle.

148

Friday of that week, employment paperwork was signed at my asking wage, with the desired hours!

This is only part-time work 3 days a week until work picks up, then possibly a full workweek. . . The offered income is before deductions, so take-home will be less than what I need (which is far less than most people are used to in our culture). But this whole thing smacks of God showing pleasure in my excitement that I could spend alone time with Him again; granting me a form of work that wasn't my first choice, but that promises adventure all on its own.

My application for Canada's Employment Insurance has the potential to be cancelled almost before it starts.

Christ says in Matthew 6:33 (KJV), *"But seek ye first the kingdom of God, and his righteousness; and all these things shall be added unto you."*

The focus is not to be on things we need, nor should our focus in seeking God be our needs. Our "me first" culture in the Church teaches that if you want your needs met, focus on God - basically saying that our motive to focus on God is so that our needs will be met. To the contrary, we should be focusing on God whether or NOT our needs are EVER met! Our motive is precisely because God is worthy of that focus. God has already done all He ever needs to do to earn our love and devotion by rescuing us from sin via His Son, Jesus Christ. It is when we take our eyes off our needs and put them onto God that God is freed to move on our behalf in whatever capacity He deems best. Our attitude should be that of Job's who said, "Though He slay me, yet will I praise Him" (see Job 13:15). God isn't required to meet our needs just because we feign to put Him first. God isn't a genie who, when rubbed the right way, gives us all that our hearts desire. Instead, the Scriptures say when we get close to God's heart, He will plant desires within us. (See Psalm 37:4)

I lost my day job when the economic climate of my city was depressed. Yet I was excited for the chance to spend time in God's presence. There has been a sense of excitement and adventure ever since. I didn't know what was going to happen or when, but it's happening and I'm tightening my seatbelt because I have no idea where this ride will stop next.

God can't help showing up when we draw near. He did promise that when we draw near to Him, He would draw near to us (see James 4:8). He can't resist those who choose to spend time with Him just for Who He is. We all want to be accepted and loved for who we are, not for what we look like or what we can do. We were formed in God's image. He feels that way too. He shows up every time we choose to love Him for being Him - No "I'm doing this so God will do that", just spending time with God for who He is.

God didn't have to bring that job along. I don't even know if this job is my final destination at this point on the journey. All I know is that God chose to honor my desire to give Him private time.

In Closing...

Shelley Hitz

In closing, I want to share two specific instances where God taught me about stepping out in faith. These include two major geographical moves where my faith was tested.

The first move, was in 2002 when we packed all of our earthly belongings into a 1988 Suburban and drove it to Belize, Central America. We ended up living there as short-term missionaries for two years. It was definitely a step of faith to quit both of our jobs, sell most of our stuff and move to a foreign country. However, on top of all of that, the Ayala's, the missionaries that would be our main contact in Belize, told us that there were currently no rental properties available for us to live in when we arrived. Therefore, we would have to live in a hotel until something opened up.

I have to admit that I didn't demonstrate the perfect picture of faith during our drive down to Belize. However, I am so thankful that God is patient with us and willing to teach us along the way. Aren't you?

Instead of trusting God to provide housing for us, I worried. Where were we going live? How long would we have to stay in a hotel? Would we have the finances necessary to stay in a hotel until a rental opened up? And the questions went on and on.

We had several delays along the way to Belize including a flat tire and other issues. So when we were finally getting ready to cross over into the Belize border, we called the Ayala's. We let them know that we would be arriving in Belize the next day. And to our surprise, they told us that a house came open

151

that very day for us to rent. They would be able to provide bedding and a few groceries for us so that we could even spend that very first night in our new house. We did not even have to spend one night in a hotel. Amazing!

However, 10 years later, we had another major move. This time we were moving to Colorado Springs, Colorado. We did not have the money at the time to fly out in advance to find a place to rent. Therefore, we did a lot of research online. Being a planner, I wanted to have a place ready to move into when we arrived in Colorado. However, my husband, CJ, wanted to actually see the place first before we signed a contract. Looking back, I am so thankful that he insisted we do it this way. But at the time, once again, I allowed worry to creep into my mind instead of trusting God to provide.

We packed all of our stuff into the moving truck and arrived in Colorado Springs on a Friday night. We needed to return the moving truck by Tuesday morning, so we had a few days to find a place to move in to or we would need to move our stuff into a storage unit in the meantime. Thankfully, a couple of realtors were willing to show us rentals over the weekend. On Sunday we visited a condo that was within our price range, in the area we wanted to live and we decided to apply to rent there. We told them our timeframe and unbelievably they were able to meet with us the next day to sign the paperwork, give us the keys and allow us to start moving in to our new place. We were completely moved in by late Monday night and were able to return the moving truck Tuesday morning and not even have to pay a late fee. Once again, God provided in an amazing way that increased my faith.

One of my heroes of the faith, Corrie ten Boom, said "Faith is like radar that sees through the fog -- the reality of things at a distance that the human eye cannot see."

How true that is! We are all on a faith journey of our own. Each day we can choose to either walk by faith or walk by sight. My prayer for myself and for you is that we learn to walk by faith.

Let me close with a prayer...

Lord, we thank You today that You are the author and perfecter of our faith. Thank You for Your patience with us on this faith journey. Empower us to keep our eyes fixed on You, Jesus, as we walk through the circumstances of life each day. Strengthen our faith in You today. We love You and praise You. In Jesus's name we pray, Amen.

Continuing a Life of Prayer

These 21 prayers are now over, but you can continue in a life of prayer. Start over at day one in this book, write out your own prayers, or get one of our other books in the series here:

21 Prayers of Gratitude
http://www.bodyandsoulpublishing.com/prayersofgratitude

21 Oraciónes de Gratitud (Spanish)
http://www.bodyandsoulpublishing.com/oracionesdegratitud

21 Prayers for Teen Girls
http://www.bodyandsoulpublishing.com/prayersforteens

Appendix

Definition of Faith:

One resource I use when studying the Bible is www.BlueLetterBible.org. Using their free online concordance, I looked up the word faith in Hebrews 11:1. Below, I have shared the definition of faith from Strong's concordance.

Pistis (Strong's G4102)
1) conviction of the truth of anything, belief; in the NT of a conviction or belief respecting man's relationship to God and divine things, generally with the included idea of trust and holy fervour born of faith and joined with it

> **a)** relating to God
> > **1)** the conviction that God exists and is the creator and ruler of all things, the provider and bestower of eternal salvation through Christ
>
> **b)** relating to Christ
> > **1)** a strong and welcome conviction or belief that Jesus is the Messiah, through whom we obtain eternal salvation in the kingdom of God
>
> **c)** the religious beliefs of Christians
> **d)** belief with the predominate idea of trust (or confidence) whether in God or in Christ, springing from faith in the same

2) fidelity, faithfulness
> **a)** the character of one who can be relied on

BONUS:
Excerpt from "A Life of Gratitude"

Want to take another challenge to continue growing in your relationship with God? Join me on a 21 days of gratitude challenge. Plus read 21 prayers of gratitude and 21 stories of gratitude on Kindle here:
http://www.amazon.com/dp/B00A8NH6R4

Read an excerpt from Day #1 below:

The Gratitude Challenge...

Thankfulness. Gratitude. Contentment.

These are words that are familiar to us...especially those of us that call ourselves followers of Jesus.

And yet, how often do we get stuck in the opposite...

Self-Pity. Complaining. Discontentment.

And I have to admit that I've been there lately. I've been through so many changes recently and some people might think that I have it made. Others might think I'm crazy. But, I don't think many realize how difficult it has been for me.

The Changes in My Life Over the Last Year

I resigned my job as a Physical Therapist last July to minister and work full time with my husband CJ. This is a dream we have been working towards ever since we came back from being short term missionaries in Belize. When we returned, we had thousands of dollars of debt which (in my thinking) forced me back to my job as a P.T. Although the job is rewarding and pays well, it was not what we felt God called us to in this season. After ministering together and working together for two years in Belize, we sensed that was what we were to continue to do.

However, seven years later, we were finally able to pay off all our consumer debt. Being debt free (except for our mortgage) allowed me to resign my job as a P.T. and embark once again into ministering and working full time together. What a great feeling it was to pay off our debt and yet the transition was harder for me than I anticipated.

I had become dependent on the regular paychecks and benefits that came with my job. And I realized that I got some of my self-worth from my job title. People instantly respected me as a "Physical Therapist" whereas I get very different reactions when I tell someone I am an "Author and Speaker". It's almost as if people want to ask, "Oh really? What's your REAL job?"

God is teaching me to gain my worth from who I am in HIM...not what I do. But, it's been a hard transition.

And then we went from living in a 1300 sq. ft. home to a 125 sq. ft. RV to living in my mom's spare bedroom to finally settling in Colorado Springs in our condo.

What a ride!

I wouldn't go back and do anything different as God used these months of transition in our lives. But, after months of living out of bags and from place to place, I was ready to "nest" again and be settled in ONE place.

When we moved out of our house into our RV, we had to get rid of a lot of stuff. If I would have known that just a few months later we would be moving into a condo in Colorado Springs, I probably would have kept some of the things I gave away. But, the experience taught me a lot about living simply. I realized that I truly didn't "need" all that material stuff. When it really came down to it, I truly only needed a very small amount of material possessions and was able to live without a lot of the stuff I thought I couldn't live without.

When we left Findlay, Ohio, it had been a place I called home for over 20 years. We moved there when I was a junior in high school in 1991 and except for college and our time in Belize, Findlay had been home. All my family lives in Ohio and so to move over 1200 miles away from my "home" was both exciting and sad.

A Season of New Things in My Life, But Also a Season of Grieving

And here I sit. Although there have been a lot of exciting changes in my life, it's also been a season of grieving.

- Grieving the loss of my job, career and what I thought I would be doing for the rest of my life.
- Grieving the loss of our first house and a lot of the material stuff that filled it.
- Grieving the loss of my "home" for 20 years and living close to my family.

And sometimes we can get stuck in the grief. God has felt distant to me throughout these changes and so sometimes I've felt alone and stuck in self-pity. Poor me. Why can't I live a "normal" life like most people?

It is Important to Grieve

And so I'm reminded that it is important to grieve…even the little things that don't seem important at the time. My mom always says it is important to feel your feelings and then let them pass, surrendering them into the hands of Jesus so that they don't get stuck or bottled up within us.

And so I have allowed myself to grieve. Even as I've written this post, I've cried a few tears. And for me, many times tears can be healing.

I Felt Stuck

And yet as I was processing some of my emotions this week I felt stuck. I've given into the habit of working long hours on both ministry and business projects. I believe workaholism is one of my last addictions from which Christ is now working to set me free.

And it's an acceptable addiction in the church and in our culture. It is even often praised.

- Great job, Shelley.
- Wow, you're a real workhorse.
- Look at all you've accomplished.

You get the picture.

It was also my way of trying – in self-sufficiency – to provide financially for our needs. I felt the burden of providing in this

159

way after I quit my P.T. job. I felt the need to replace the income I was giving up when I resigned my job but also wanted to do whatever I needed to do to ensure that I wouldn't need to work a "9 to 5" kind of job again. I wanted to have the freedom to continue to minister with CJ as God opens the doors as well as work from home when, in God's timing, we start a family. We are praying that this happens sooner rather than later, but again trusting God's timing.

Self-sufficiency and workaholism run rampant in our culture, I believe.

It's so easy to get caught up in the rat race. We keep ourselves so busy. Even after resigning my job as a P.T. there were often many times I would work 12 hour days. I am very driven and yet I joked with CJ that I was working harder than I ever did in my P.T. job.

Praying for Freedom and Contentment

And so here I am. Praying for freedom from the unbalanced life I created. Praying for freedom from the self-sufficiency and workaholism deeply rooted in my life. Praying for contentment in my circumstances.

And then this week I had a friend email me and say she was praying for accountability in a certain area and the only person that came to her mind was me. I agreed to do so for her and asked if she would also help keep me accountable in my workaholism and living a more balanced life. She agreed and I believe God is providing for both of us in this way. Even though we are thousands of miles apart, we are keeping each other accountable via email on a daily basis and praying for each other. God has provided accountability for me in other areas of my life just when I needed it and I believe He is providing it for me again.

A Reminder of One of Our Greatest Weapons as Christians...a Spirit of Thankfulness and Gratitude

Another thing God kept bringing to my mind this week is thankfulness and gratitude. I was reminded that thankfulness and gratitude are the opposite of self-pity and a complaining spirit.

I know, I know. It seems like a pat answer. "Just be thankful for what you have." "Give thanks in all things." But, there is POWER in being thankful...even when you don't FEEL like being thankful.

I remembered a book I started to read in a Barnes and Noble bookstore one day about a man who began to write thank you notes every day for one year. It wasn't a Christian book but demonstrated the power in being intentionally thankful. I believe it is a Biblical concept that can be experienced by anyone who practices it.

And then I remembered people who I've seen post on Facebook or their blogs something they are thankful for everyday for a series of days. I felt led to do something similar and remembered that...

It Takes 21 Days to Start a New Habit

Many people say it takes 21 days to start a new habit or break an old one. Whether it is getting in the habit of exercising, eating right or developing a spirit of thankfulness.

And so I decided to take a 21 Day Gratitude Challenge. I hope you'll join me.

However, the gratitude challenge was just my first step. The next step was the 21 prayers of gratitude.

161

Prayers of Gratitude

Prayer changes things. It changes me. When I pray consistently to God something changes within me. However, sometimes it is easy to get caught up in the busyness of life and not take the time to pray.

We do not have to pray in a certain way for God to hear us. We can simply lift up the prayer of our hearts to Him as if we are talking with a friend. However, in this book, I have taken key truths from scripture and reworded them into prayers of gratitude. Combining prayer with God's Word is powerful. I have experienced this in my own life and now want to share it with you.

They say it takes 21 days to form a new habit. And so I have shared 21 prayers of gratitude with you to help you form a habit of prayer in your life. I pray that these prayers help you to overcome negativity through applying the power of prayer and God's Word to your life. I also pray that when you finish this book, your prayers will continue on your own. I encourage you to dig into God's Word and come up with your own prayers. If you are struggling in a certain area, I recommend using a concordance or an online tool like BibleGateway.com or BlueLetterBible.org to find scriptures on that topic and then reword them into prayers from your own heart.

"Pray without ceasing."
~ I Thessalonians 5:17

"Ask, and it will be given to you; seek, and you will find; knock, and it will be opened to you."
~ Matthew 7:7

"Be anxious for nothing, but in everything by prayer and supplication, with thanksgiving, let Your requests be made known to God; 7 and the peace of God, which surpasses all understanding, will guard Your hearts and minds through Christ Jesus."

~ Philippians 4:6-7

And finally, God led me to compile 21 stories of gratitude to provide encouragement and inspiration.

Stories of Gratitude

"If you look at the world, you'll be distressed. If you look within, you'll be depressed. But if you look at Christ, you'll be at rest."

~ Corrie ten Boom

What a great quote by one of my heroes of the faith, Corrie ten Boom. She was a Nazi prison camp survivor and knew what it was like to go through difficult circumstances in life. However, as we share in one of the stories later in this book, Corrie and her sister Betsie found out that it is possible to live life with a grateful heart. They displayed gratitude even when living amongst some of the worst circumstances we can imagine.

How about you? Are you living life to the fullest? Or are you merely surviving from day to day?

One way to live life to the fullest is to live each day with a grateful heart. In this book, we share 21 stories of gratitude to give you encouragement and hope in your own journey. Gratitude is possible! Even though many times we cannot change our circumstances, we can change the way we see them. We can ask God to empower us to change our thoughts. Beth Moore explains this well in a quote from her Patriarchs study, *"I have been told many times, 'Beth, I can't change the way I feel.' But we can change the way we think, which will lead to a change in the way we feel. That's the essences of the renewed mind."*

Our prayer for you is that you find encouragement within these pages. And we pray that you will ask God for His strength to renew your mind with His truth and the hope He offers each one of us every day. It is only through Christ renewing our minds that we can truly live each day with a grateful heart.

"And do not be conformed to this world, but be transformed by the renewing of your mind, that you may prove what is that good and acceptable and perfect will of God."

~ Romans 12:2

Other Resources:

Here are some resources that you might be interested in during this gratitude challenge (and even beyond)...

> http://thankfulfor.com - free private or public gratitude journal online
>
> http://itunes.apple.com/us/app/gratitude-journal-for-ipad/id402667476 - $1.99 gratitude journal for iPhone/iPad
>
> https://play.google.com/store/apps/details?id=no.vista media.grattitude - free attitude of gratitude Android app

Are You Ready to Get Started?

Let's start with a prayer...

Lord I thank You for each person who will read this book. I pray that You would do a mighty work in their hearts as they spend these next 21 days focused on Your spirit of gratitude in their lives. Change them from the inside out through this challenge, Your Word and prayer. Give them a hunger and thirst for You that will continue past the last page of this book. And replace any negativity and self-pity in their lives with a spirit of gratitude that comes from You. Amen.

Day #1

21 Days of Gratitude...

What does this mean? It can mean different things for different people. But, for me, I sense that I need to take the initiative to write down the things and people in my life that I am grateful for in my journal for the next 21 days. At the same time, I will choose one person each day to write a hand-written thank you note to them. In the note, I will share why I am thankful for them and send it via postal mail.

I found 21 thank you notes and cards in my closet, got them out and wrote my first thank you note today.

Then, I got out my journal – that has been somewhat neglected over the past few months – and wrote out three specific things that I am thankful for in my life today in these three categories: spiritual, physical and relational. I wrote several sentences of what I am thankful for and why in each category.

And already I can feel the direction of my heart changing. Imagine what will happen after 21 days of being intentionally thankful for all I've been given.

Because I've been given a lot…more than I deserve.

And it's time to not allow Satan to keep me in the grips of self-pity, a complaining attitude and discontentment. I am asking God to break through in my heart through the power of His Holy Spirit as I take these intentional steps toward gratitude.

Will You Join Me?

What about you? Will you consider joining me in these 21 Days of Gratitude? It may look different for you and that's okay. Simply ask God what He wants you to do and then do it. It may be as simple as saying out loud one thing you are thankful for each day. Or like me, you may decide to write out thank you notes.

If you feel stuck in self-pity or discontentment, I challenge you to join me. Ask the Holy Spirit to change you as you take simple steps of intentional gratitude in your life. And watch and see what God does.

"Appreciation is the highest form of prayer, for it acknowledges the presence of good wherever you shine the light of your thankful thoughts."

~ Alan Cohen

Psalm 100:4, *"Enter into His gates with thanksgiving, And into His courts with praise. Be thankful to Him, and bless His name."*

The Gratitude Challenge:

❖ If you're ready to take this challenge with me and want to share the journey with others, join our private Facebook group here:
www.bodyandsoulpublishing.com/gratitudegroup

Once you are there, I encourage you to post something you are grateful for each day for 21 days. You can also post stories of how God is working in your life through the gratitude challenge.

❖ Or buy a notebook and journal and write what you are grateful for each day in it. That's what I did. I chose three categories to write something I'm thankful for each day: spiritual, physical and relational. I also wrote a handwritten thank you card to someone different each day of my 21 days of gratitude challenge.

❖ Whatever, you do, I encourage you to spend time focusing on all that God has given you.

Prayer of Gratitude:
Grace

Lord, today I want to thank You for Your grace. Grace is simply getting something good I do not deserve. So many times I take Your grace for granted, please forgive me. Open my eyes to see Your grace more clearly in my life. Lord, I ask that You take the blinders off of my spiritual eyes so that I can see all of the gifts You have so graciously given me.

It is by Your grace ALONE that I am saved from eternal punishment and have the promise that I will be with You in heaven for eternity one day. Thank You for rescuing me from my sin and from the clutches of the evil one, Satan. You died for me so that I could have life and life abundantly. Thank You for Your sacrifice.

Thank You for giving me life each new day. When I wake up in the morning, empower me to focus my first thoughts on You. As I lay my head on the pillow at night, remind me of all that You have given me that day. Show me the gifts You have given me and empower me to say a simple, "Thank You" back to You.

Thank You for Your amazing grace. Without it, I would be in a hopeless situation. But, because of Your grace, I have so much to be thankful for today…and every day.

I love You, Lord. Amen.

"Every good gift and every perfect gift is from above, and comes down from the Father of lights, with whom there is no variation or shadow of turning."
~ James 1:17

"For by grace you have been saved through faith, and that not of yourselves; it is the gift of God."
~ Ephesians 2:8

"The thief does not come except to steal, and to kill, and to destroy. I have come that they may have life, and that they may have it more abundantly."
~ John 10:10

"May grace (God's favor) and peace (which is perfect well-being, all necessary good, all spiritual prosperity, and freedom from fears and agitating passions and moral conflicts) be multiplied to you in [the full, personal, precise, and correct] knowledge of God and of Jesus our Lord."
~ 2 Peter 1:2 (AMP)

Story of Gratitude:
Changed From Within

Heather Hart

"Let the peace of Christ rule in your hearts, since as members of one body you were called to peace. And be thankful."
~ Colossians 3:15 (NIV)

When I first began thinking of a gratitude story to share, I honestly could not think of one. However, after some prayerful contemplation I realized that the reason I could not think of a specific way gratitude has impacted my life, was because it has done so in such a complete way.

You see, several years ago I went through a Revive Our Hearts 30-Day Husband Encouragement Challenge. While I don't remember them ever using the word gratitude to describe what they were teaching us, that is exactly what I got out of it. They encouraged us to not say anything negative to our husbands or about our husbands for 30 days - thus they encouraged us to choose gratitude.

This was in the first years of my marriage. My husband and I were raising four children together, two boys from a previous marriage and our newborn twin girls. As only one of the four was old enough for school, I had to quit my job and become a full time stay at home mommy - there simply were not any jobs that could pay enough to cover the cost of day care for

169

three children - and I was miserable. The only adult I ever saw was my husband. He was coming home from working 12 hour shifts at his job, exhausted, only to encounter a wife that was stressed to the max, and looking for someone to blame and take over. Looking back, I most certainly don't envy what he went through, and have been thanking God ever since for saving my marriage.

Throughout the 30-days of learning to be grateful for my husband, not only did my marriage improve, but my walk with God grew to an entire new level. I started seeing Him in a new way. He wanted me to choose gratitude and thank Him for what He had blessed me with - even when the twins were crying. Even when I hadn't slept for more than an hour at a time in the past 3 months. Even when my husband wasn't reading my mind. Even when the house was a disaster.

Choosing gratitude helped me to see things in a whole new light. It was no longer about where I was, or what was happening in the moment. It was about what I had, and what God had done for me. No, my husband is not perfect, but neither am I. My kids don't always listen, and my house still isn't clean - but God has taught me to be grateful for my life anyway. To be thankful for my wonderful children, and that we have a place to live.

I still have days where the depression sinks in, but God always brings me back to His peace and reminds me of what He has given me. Moreover, even when I'm in the throes of life, I am grateful that my family and my God love me enough to stick with me through it all.

This was an excerpt from the Book, *"A Life of Gratitude: 21 Days to Overcoming Self-Pity and Negativity."*

Continue reading and join me in this gratitude challenge here:
http://www.amazon.com/dp/B00A8NH6R4

Prefer print?

"A Life of Gratitude" makes a great gift. Get the paperback version here:
http://www.amazon.com/dp/0615731260

About the Authors

Story of Faith Contributors

CJ Hitz - CJ is an author, speaker and entrepreneur. In his downtime, he enjoys spending time outdoors running, hiking and exploring God's beautiful creation. You can find his books at www.BodyAndSoulPublishing.com

Mikayla Kayne - Mikayla currently lives in Rochester, NY with her co-writer husband, Gregory Kayne, and their three sons. They are active in ministry, both speaking and leading worship for camps and special events. You can find them at www.kaynecreative.com.

Mary L. Ball - Mary L. Ball is a published author of Inspirational Romantic Suspense and Mystery. Her novels inspire the enchantment of love, hope and a divine guidance that often lies dormant, waiting to be found by each of us. She often tackles subjects not common in Christian fiction. Nevertheless the subjects are shared by everyone in life. Writing Christian Articles keeps her focused on the real meaning of life. Contact her and find more about her books at http://MaryLouwrites.weebly.com.

Nishoni Harvey - Nishoni Harvey is a saved, sanctified, and soul winning Baptist. She, her husband, Matthew, and their 3 young children serve faithfully at Hope Baptist Church of Harrison, Michigan, where they're active members. A graduate of Landmark Baptist College, Nishoni loves teaching, writing, playing with her instruments, and being a mommy. Nishoni is the author of THE FANATICS, which can be found at:
www.amazon.com/gp/aw/d/B009XV1KEC

Ruth Kyser - Ruth Kyser is the author of several Christian fiction novels: "True Cover", "Endless Season", and "The Dove & The Raven". She enjoys telling stories that share how much God loves us.

You can connect with her on-line at her blog:
http://ruthkyser.wordpress.com
Or Facebook at: http://www.facebook.com/authorruth.kyser

Krystal Kuehn - Krystal Kuehn, MA, LPC, LLP, NCC is a psychotherapist, best-selling author, teacher, musician and songwriter. Krystal specializes in helping people live their best life now, reach their full potential, overcome barriers, heal from their past, & develop a happiness lifestyle. Her inspirational and empowering approach has been helping people all over the world for over 20 years. Her books, articles, poetry, and songs have been published locally and internationally. Krystal has a passion for encouraging others. She believes everyone has untapped potential for greatness, and everyone can live a life of fulfillment and true happiness. Krystal is the co-founder of New Day Counseling in Michigan.

Her web sites include: www.BeHappy4Life.com,
www.NewDayCounseling.org,
www.NewSongProductions.com,
www.Baby-Poems.com as well as
www.Facebook.com/WordsOfInspiration,
and Be Your Best blog
http://www.newdaycounselingcenter.blogspot.com.

Cliff Ball - Cliff Ball is a born again Christian and is a member of his local Baptist church. Cliff first became published in high school in the early 90's, and has published nine novels and two short stories. Please visit his website at www.cliffball.net.

Ada Brownell - Ada Brownell has written for Christian publications since age 15 and spent much of her life as a newspaper reporter. She is the author of the teen novel Joe the Dreamer: The Castle and the Catapult - http://buff.ly/XeqTvH; and Swallowed by LIFE: Mysteries of Death, Resurrection and the Eternal - http://amzn.to/Jnc1rW.

Amanda Penland - Amanda is a stay-at-home mom of five, house wife, Body and Soul Publishing Blog Manager, and Blogger at http://LordLeadMeOn.blogspot.com.

Janet Perez Eckles - Best-selling author and international speaker, Janet Perez Eckles offers personal success coaching. Your free, 30-minute coaching session with her is just a click away: www.janetperezeckles.com.

Jorja Davis - Jorja Davis is a retired librarian and teacher. Her chronic pain leaves her plenty of time to read, write reviews, blog, and quilt. God seems always to send people to nurture. Today her greatest joy is daughters who encourage her to be deeply involved in the lives and faith of their children.
http://jorjaadavisthewriterreads.blogspot.com
http://jorjaadaviscommonprayer.blogspot.com
http://jorjaadavisnana911.blogspot.com

Kim Bookmyer - Kim Bookmyer is a wife, mother, daughter, sister, friend BUT most importantly a daughter of the King!

Mark Moyers - Mark is a minister, a mentor, a leader and more. Called by God at an early age, Mark has walked a long and difficult road few have chosen to travel. If there is a hallmark of Mark's life and ministry, it is his desire to help people live free and receive all God has for them.

Read more stories about Mark's journey with God and the insights God has given him in his book, "Who Is This God

174

Anyway?: One Man's Pursuit of God and the Wonders He Discovered (2013)" Find it and more at: WhoIsThisGodAnyway.com.

Lilly Maytree - Lilly Maytree is an inspirational adventure novelist who is living out her dreams aboard the GLORY B. You can follow along with her by visiting http://www.LillysArmchairTravelers.blogspot.com.

A list of her books is available at www.LillyMaytree.com.

Carol Freed - Over 45 years of marriage, raising three sons, volunteering in my community, church and schools has given me endless opportunities to see things as they could be and do the unusual and unexpected. I have two web sites to encourage Christians worldwide and published an eBook in 2012 "Encourage-Mints."

Laura J. Marshall - Laura J. Marshall is the full-time mother of five sons and part-time writer and blogger. She operates a popular blog called The Old Stone Wall. Laura writes devotionals and inspirational romantic suspense. A Mom's Battle Cry to Overcome Fear , the second book in her best-selling Battle Cry Devotional Series, has just released. Visit www.LauraJMarshall.com to find out more about Laura's books.

Cheryl Rogers - Cheryl Rogers came to know Christ as an adult after succumbing to a severe immune disorder and surrendering her life to Him. A former newspaper reporter, she has dedicated herself to sharing the good news of Christ through her writing. She writes eBooks and publishes New Christian Books Online Magazine: http://www.songsfromtheword.com/NewChristianBooks.

Carol McCormick - Carol has been a speaker for Christian Women's Connection (Stonecroft Ministries International) for over 15 years. She is also an international bestselling author who has appeared on regional and Christian television programs and has been a guest on over fifty Christian and secular radio stations.

You can find out more about Carol McCormick and her books at…
www.amazon.com/author/carolmccormick and
http://www.carolmccormick.com.

Victor Brodt - Author, Artist, and Speaker. He especially loves to tell stories about a famous old dog named Jack. They're parables and reflections of Jesus and God's love for you. Despite great challenges, Victor and his wife are encouragers and ministers to the core. Google his unique name.

Rev. Paul B. Heidt - Lead Pastor of Living Hope Assembly of God. Hamlin, New York

Marilynn Dawson - Marilynn lives with her two teenagers, cat and gerbil, in Canada. In the evenings and on weekends she's a sound tech doing various events through the year from funerals to workshops to concerts and weddings. Marilynn sings in the choir and sang on her church's praise teams for several years.

Get Free Christian Books

Love getting FREE Christian books online? If so, sign up to get notified of new Christian book promotions and never miss out. Then, grab a cup of coffee and enjoy reading the free Christian books you download.

You will also get our FREE report, *"How to Find Free Christian Books Online"* that shows you 7 places you can get new books…for free!

Sign up at: www.bodyandsoulpublishing.com/freebooks

Happy reading!

Contact Information:

We would love to hear from you! Send me an e-mail to the following address: shelley@shelleyhitz.com

Websites:

www.bodyandsoulpublishing.com
www.shelleyhitz.com

CJ and Shelley Hitz

CJ and Shelley Hitz enjoy sharing God's Truth through their speaking engagements and their writing. On downtime, they enjoy spending time outdoors running, hiking and exploring God's beautiful creation.

To find out more about their ministry check out their website at www.BodyandSoulPublishing.com or to invite them to your next event go to www.ChristianSpeakers.tv.

Note from the Author: Reviews are gold to authors! If you have enjoyed this book, would you consider reviewing it on Amazon.com? Thank you!

Other Books by Shelley Hitz

A Life of Gratitude

Trusting God When Bad Things Happen

Forgiveness Formula

Unshackled and Free

Body Image Lies Women Believe

Mirror Mirror… Am I Beautiful?

Teen Devotionals… for Girls!

See the entire list here: www.ShelleyHitz.com